Haynes

Dance

Manual

First published in September 2016

British Library Cataloguing in Publication Data
A catalogue record for this book is available
from the British Library.

ISBN 978 1 78521 062 4

Library of Congress catalog card no. 2016930192

Published by Haynes Publishing,
Sparkford, Yeovil, Somerset BA22 7JJ, UK
Tel: 01963 440635
Int. tel: +44 1963 440635
Website: www.haynes.com

Haynes North America Inc.
861 Lawrence Drive, Newbury Park,
California 91320, USA

Printed and bound in Malaysia

Author:	Keyna Paul
Project Manager:	Louise McIntyre
Copy editor:	Beth Dymond
Design:	Richard Parsons
Photography:	Nathan Pidd
Stock photos:	Shutterstock, Getty
Video:	Nathan Pidd and Kashilembo Wabu
Video music:	AKM Music,
	Bollywood music from South Star Music

Author's Acknowledgements

The author thanks **Pat Sharkey** (Fellow IDTA): A professional dancer, teacher and competition adjudicator
across the UK and Europe, for his input with the text and photographs in the book relating to American
Line Dance and the waltz. I particularly would like to thank him for taking on the challenge of teaching
me to waltz in six lessons.

    Guillermo Torrens and **Maria Maragaki**: Dancers in the West End Show Midnight Tango and Winner
of Latin-UK Awards (LUKAS) 2011 and 2012 for Best Tango Performers and Teachers, for sharing their
knowledge of Argentine Tango and modelling for the photographs. Additional thanks to Maria for her
work on the flamenco section.

    Katrina Brackenbury: A professional dancer who performed internationally for over ten years before
focusing on teaching, for sharing her knowledge particularly in Bollywood and Burlesque dance and for
modelling for many of the pictures. I am grateful to her for the enthusiasm and laughter that she has
brought to this process.

    Thanks also to Judy and Sarah for reading the text and trying out the exercises and, of course, to Jon.

Haynes

Dance
Manual

The complete
step-by-step guide

Keyna Paul

Contents

Introduction

Attitudes to dance have changed considerably over the past decade. Dance has increased in popularity and, as a leisure activity, has moved beyond the preserve of the young and fit.

It is gaining recognition as a way for everyone to improve and maintain their physical health including losing weight, maintaining strong bones and improving posture and balance. In addition, there is a growing agreement that dance gives us a sense of well-being, through the physical activity itself and the increased confidence and socialisation it offers.

According to the NHS website more than 4.8 million people regularly attend community dance groups each year in England. Many more adults, however, would like to attend dance classes but do not for many reasons, mainly because of confusion about different styles and fear of looking foolish.

This book gives you a chance to try out some dance styles at home and to find one, or several, that you can enjoy. It provides a simple explanation of the dance styles, gets you started with practice tasks that include popular steps from the genre and finishes with a short dance sequence. Once you have mastered the basics there are some more challenging steps to help you develop further.

The accompanying video has the moving version of the dance sequences for the beginner and more advanced dancer in each style. Use the breakdown of steps in the book and look at the video to see how they work together in the sequence and check how you are doing.

It takes a while to learn to dance, so don't give up if you don't get the moves right first time. Keep practising or return to the warm-up exercises, which will help you gain more strength, flexibility and co-ordination. The book also includes a seated section to show how people with physical limitations can enjoy and be supported to enjoy dance. If you are thinking about starting dance, or want to explore some different styles then this is the book for you.

How to use this book

If you are fit and active or have danced before, you will probably find it easy to just dive in and get started. if you are less fit or more wary of dance, do the warm ups until you feel confident and in control of your movements.

The steps

◆ The steps and movements for the exercises and sequences are written and supported by photographs.
◆ There are slight variations in how things are written in different styles, due to the nature of those styles and established traditions, but the same format is used as much as possible.
◆ In partner dances, the terms leader and follower are used for the traditional male and female roles. The leader's steps are written in purple and the follower's in green.

Videos

Watch the video before you try the sequence so that you can see how the steps fit together and any changes in direction made by the dancer.

▶️ Watch the video
Haynes.com/dancemanual

Music

◆ It is recommended that the practice tasks for each style are initially carried out without music so that you can focus fully on how your body is working. If it helps, it can be fun to count the beat out loud as you dance so you can feel the rhythm, although if you are counting unaccompanied, you need to be careful not to speed up or slow down!
◆ Pieces of music are suggested for each specific dance style to get you started and give an idea of the best time signature and tempo for the tasks and sequences. Play this quietly in the background for the practice tasks, so that it influences but does not dominate your movements.

Counting the beat

Finding the beat and rhythm of each dance helps get the timing of the movement right. It helps the dance to flow, look smooth and work seamlessly with the music. Often, at the beginning, counting and dancing is a challenge, but as you try more dance styles it will become easier. Have a go at counting the beat, but if it's too difficult to start with, just concentrate on the movements. As you gain confidence in how you do the steps and relax, counting the beat will become easier and you can revisit this section then. To help with consistency, throughout the book:

◆ The first count of a phrase is replaced with the number of phrases used in the sequence so far. This means in three phrases of music (or dance) with eight counts in a phrase we get:

First phrase:	12345678
Second phrase:	22345678
Third phrase:	32345678

◆ When a movement happens between the beats in a phrase, the ampersand (&) is used. So in three phrases of music (or dance) with eight counts in a phrase we get:

First phrase:	&1&2&3&4&5&6&7&8
Second phrase:	&2&2&3&4&5&6&7&8
Third phrase:	&3&2&3&4&5&6&7&8

Going in the right direction

As a dancer it is important to know precisely where you are in a room and the direction in which you are going to dance. This will help you remember the dance steps. It will also mean that if more than one person is dancing in the same room, they will be able to move easily within the space without colliding into each other.

To help with consistency, throughout the book:

◆ Changes of direction usually occur in the sequences, so use the film to help you to orientate yourself, as well as the photographs and text.
◆ For consistency, spatial directions are given in relation to your position in the room. Imagine you are standing in the middle of a room. The way that you are facing is the front of the room (or front of the stage). Any directions given in the text are written as if you are standing in this position, as shown in the table below:

Right corner, back of room	Back of room	Left corner, back of room
Right side	YOU ARE HERE	Left side
Right corner, front of room	Front of room	Left corner, front of room

◆ Diagrams of feet are sometimes used under the photographs to help you to identify changes in direction taken by dancers in the sequences.
◆ The waltz contains many changes in direction, so the numbers on a traditional clock face are used alongside the feet diagrams for additional support.

Five useful instructions

1 Choose a dance style that suits your level of fitness.

2 You could even start with the section at the end, Adapting dance for sitting on a chair (see page 182).

3 Explore the dance styles in any order, but study the essential information and work through the practice tasks in order before trying out the sequence.

4 Keep repeating the tasks to refine your technique.

5 Most of all, whether you are on your own or with a few friends, give it a go!

Abbreviations

Abbreviations are traditionally used when writing dance patterns and figures. This book tries to find a balance between using abbreviations and keeping meaning in the instructions for people who are not used to reading dance scripts. Body parts are always written in full, except in some styles where RF and LF are used. Throughout the book, the following abbreviations may be used:

bwd	Backward
bhd	Behind
C	Centre
EP	End position
fwd	Forward
X4	Four times
frt	Front
L	Left
LF	Left foot
LHS	Left hand side
LOD	Line of dance
PP	Promenade position
rpt	Repeat
rtn	Return
R	Right
RF	Right foot
SP	Starting position
X	Stillness/silence

What is dance?

Dance is movement that speaks to us. It threads through history, influencing and being influenced by things that happen right up to the time that we live in today.

Dance has taken many different roles and pathways, developing differently across the world, depending on the religious beliefs, social structures and economic traditions of individual nations and entire regions.

As far as we know, people have always danced. The aboriginal people in Australia passed on stories through 'Dreamtime', singing songs and dancing. Wall paintings in Egyptian tombs show people dancing on occasions such as celebratory feasts, funerals and coronations. Ancient Greek artefacts show people dancing to their gods and the great Greek Dramas included dance undertaken by a chorus to strengthen the messages they carried.

Capoeira, which to watch seems to be a blend of martial arts and dance, is believed to have evolved in Brazil where slaves used it as a way to train and retain fighting skills. Presenting it as dance was to mislead the Portuguese plantation owners about its real purpose. Capoeira is a good example of how some dance styles have developed through adversity as a way of keeping a cultural identity.

Flamenco is another such dance form. It is generally accepted that the melancholy rhythms and songs gave the gypsy communities in Southern Spain a sense of identity, especially during the 18th century when strict laws were used to supress their culture.

Traditional Egyptian wall painting showing a band of female musicians and young dancers during a funerary banquet of the 18th dynasty (circa 1390).

Industrialisation and travel have had a huge influence in changing societies and how people dance. In England, during the industrial revolution, people took folk dances from their villages into the cities, evolving dance styles to fit with the changing society. Clog dancing developed through workers mimicking the rhythms of the machines in the large industrial mills in the north-west to relieve their boredom. As the 'Grand Tour' of Europe became popular with the British upper classes during the 19th century, dances such as the waltz came to Great Britain via the fashionable court of Paris.

The more people travelled, the more dances were transported from one country to another and styles changed and evolved, sometimes emerging as completely new dance styles. One of the biggest influences on the evolution of dance styles was the transportation of people from West African countries to the Caribbean and southern states of America during the slave trade. Tap, jazz and several types of street dance, which all evolved in the USA, have their roots in dance from West Africa.

The 'Dance Off' typical of street dance is not new, merely a renaming of the 'duel' that was central to the way tap dancers learned and developed their skills. This was immortalised in the vaudeville acts of the early 1920s. In fact, it can be traced back to the southern slave plantations in the mid 18th century, and the Cake Walk; a competitive dance where the winning couple were awarded a cake, hence the name.

Individual steps can also be traced back through history. Despite popular belief, 'Twerking' did not start with Miley Cyrus in 2013 or Beyoncé in 2005, nor the New Orleans Bounce music in the 1990s or the black bottom flapper dance in the 1920s. The roots of twerking can be traced back to traditional dances from West Africa, such as the Mapouka. Likewise, inspiration for Michael Jackson's Moonwalk, which he first famously performed in 1983 (where he moved backwards but appeared to be walking forwards), combined the gliding technique from Funk Popping style, which emerged from the West Coast of America in the 1970s and the Cake Walk.

Mass migration by Punjabis following partition in 1947 introduced Bhangra, an energetic folk dance, to many countries. Bollywood films continue to bring the rich and diverse dance background of the Indian subcontinent to

Dancer performing the Cake Walk, circa 1903.

Two woman dancing the Mapouka, a traditional west African dance which has inspired dances such as the Black Bottom and Twerking.

an international audience. Early films used Bharatanatyam, Kathak and Kathakali (often now referred to collectively as the classical styles), which traditionally had a deep religious significance fused with energetic folk styles such as Bhangra. Since embracing disco in the 1970s, Bollywood continues to blend traditional styles with an ever increasing range of other styles including jazz, hip hop, Arabic and Latin forms. Bollywood dance is now a craze that has swept across the world, not only raising the profile of the film industry but also achieving a life of its own.

Technology has a growing influence on how social and theatre dance forms change and develop. One way that this can be easily seen is how performing companies, particularly in contemporary dance, are using lighting. It is no longer just a way to ensure the performers are seen on stage, or give a hint as to the mood of the dance – now technology can make lighting an equal partner in the performance. Michael Hull, a lighting designer, has collaborated with artists including Russell Maliphant and Akram Khan to explore ways of mixing light and movement. Pixel (2014), a collaboration between Mourad Merouki, Claire Bardainne and Adrien Mondot, integrates lighting and dancers so they appear to react to each other, almost as if the lighting is another dancer, or several dancers on the stage. Technology also

enables dance companies to design virtual sets and costumes, as well as recording performances.

For people interested in dance and learning to dance, the Internet has opened up a wealth of knowledge with networks and forums offering a huge range of information about events to attend, along with the latest news about different dance styles. These networks and forums also offer the chance for dancers to connect, enabling them to share ideas and moves. YouTube has an almost endless number of demonstrations and instructions for how to dance as well as performances or extracts of performances by professional companies. Technology also made the creation of the dance mat possible – an electronic game controller operated by the feet. Originally an arcade game, dance mats have proven to be more than a fad and remain very popular both for commercial and home use.

Dance in the 21st century is exciting. Greater diversity in cultures, easier access to dance styles through technology and growth of informal learning from peers is keeping dance fresh and vibrant. In the UK, popular television programmes such as *Strictly Come Dancing* and *Britain's Got Talent* have sparked people's interest in dance and inspire many people to start dancing each year. One thing is certain, dance will continue to be influenced by events in the world and be changed by them.

The benefits of dancing

Dance can improve; posture, balance, maintain strong bones, help with weight loss and be great fun. It is also recognised as helping us to age healthily and can play a role in managing some long-term and life-limiting conditions.

The health of a person is generally seen as having two parts:

1 **Physical health:** this includes the fitness of an individual, dependent on the condition of the heart, lungs, blood, blood vessels and muscles.

2 **Well-being:** this includes feeling comfortable with who you are, being confident and happy.

Dancing makes a contribution to both aspects of health. Not only does it improve your physical fitness but it also helps you to feel at home in your body, increasing your awareness of it and how you can control it. Dance is often seen as a social activity that can be experienced for the joy of movement to music rather than an exercise and a chore. Dancing is more than just steps and patterns; it's about sharing your soul and finding out who you are – whichever style you choose.

As we age, dance brings additional benefits. The use of steps and patterns is thought to help maintain memory and develop neural pathways in the brains of older dancers. Good posture puts less strain on joints and does not stress the ligaments, tendons and muscles; meaning less of those annoying niggles and physically limiting ailments such as bad knees, hips and backs. Muscle strength and good balance helps to reduce falls and (as importantly) the fear of falling.

The medical profession is gradually starting to acknowledge the role that dance can play in managing long-term and life-limiting conditions in terms of both physical fitness and well-being.

Dance

- ◆ Offers you a way to improve your strength and flexibility, which helps keep muscles and joints healthy.
- ◆ Helps you learn about your body, improving your posture, balance and co-ordination.
- ◆ Can increase your stamina and cardiovascular health.
- ◆ Keeps both your body and brain active, vital for people of every age.
- ◆ Helps reduce your stress levels as you create time for yourself.
- ◆ Helps reduce depression, as well as increase your self-esteem and confidence through mastering new skills.
- ◆ Offers a creative outlet for you to express your personality in a safe environment.
- ◆ Is a fun way to open up new possibilities, keep healthy and enjoy yourself!

Conditions helped by dancing

Parkinson's disease

People living with Parkinson's disease start to find movements that we think of as automatic and natural difficult. Research shows that learning to dance helps the brain to create new neural pathways so the body remembers how to undertake these moves. Improved muscle strength and memory, plus greater control and mobility of feet, ankles, knees and legs gained by dancing help with balance and transferring of weight. You would be amazed how often we use these skills in everyday life. It is also thought that using music for dance gives an external stimulus, helping to initiate movement and therefore giving a freedom to moving that is not there for those living with Parkinson's disease.

Osteoarthritis

Osteoarthritis develops through wear and tear of joints. Bone spurs form, misshaping the joint and leading to a lot of pain and so sufferers tend to avoid moving. Low-impact dance styles, such as line dancing and circle dancing, help to keep joints working as much as possible, for as long as possible, therefore maintaining muscle strength, flexibility and cardio endurance.

Osteoporosis

Strong bones mean that we are less likely to suffer a break or fracture if we fall. Our bone density reaches its peak when we are 35 years old, so it is important to be active when we are young. It is also important to keep doing weight-bearing exercises as we age to maintain and lessen the loss of our bone density as much as possible. Dance is an ideal way to exercise, as dancers change the position of their weight and change directions a lot in a short period of time. Dance has the additional benefit of helping with balance and co-ordination, reducing the chances of falling in the first place.

Dementia

Dementia is a general term for loss of memory and other mental abilities to a level that impacts on everyday life. Research has shown that the new neural pathways developed by dancing can delay the onset of dementia and are helpful during its early stages. Partner dances, such as ballroom or sequence dance, appear to be particularly beneficial. This may be because as well as listening to music and remembering steps, dancing with a partner needs you to accommodate their movements, as well as your own, so involves the brain on yet another level. Interest is growing in the role dance as a non-verbal form of communication can play within dementia therapies.

Each of us is unique and it is important that if you have any of these conditions, other health issues, or have led a very sedentary lifestyle that you consult your doctor before trying any of the dance styles in this book. Why not take this book along to your next appointment with your GP and discuss what you want to do with them?

Which style to choose

Each dance style combine the five basic elements in different ways creating a distinct feel. It is exciting to try out a few styles spotting the similarities and differences before studying one in more depth.

People decide they want to dance for different reasons. Some of the most common are to:

◆ Recapture the joy they had learning to dance as a child.
◆ Fulfil a long-held dream of learning to dance.
◆ Get physically fit, either just to have a healthier lifestyle or perhaps after a health scare or injury.
◆ Have a distraction and stress reliever from the complexities of life.
◆ Make time to be creative.
◆ Have fun and make new friends.
◆ Challenge themselves after a change in personal circumstances or from being inspired by a film or television series, such as *Strictly Come Dancing*.

When people talk of sport it is used as an umbrella title, including activities such as football and rugby as well as tennis, athletics, darts and bowls. Dance, too, is an umbrella title covering many different styles. Just as people often try lots of different sports before finding one they really like (or rejecting it altogether!), so it should be with dance. If you find one type of dance doesn't suit you, try another – don't assume that you can't dance! Each dance style has its own unique characteristics, flavour, dress and shoe needs. This book focuses on ten popular styles of dance easily accessible in local classes, on television, on the Internet or in films.

Deciding which dance style to try can be a bit like buying a house. How many people have you heard say about a house they have purchased or rented, 'I walked through the door and felt at home, I knew it was the one for me'? Often that house is not the first they'd visited; and it can be the same trying to find a dance style that you enjoy – you may need to try a few out before you find the one that suits you.

Which style to choose?

People are different; some people like living in cities with all of the noise and the hustle and bustle of urban life, while others prefer the space and more natural rhythms of the countryside. Some people like to holiday alone, some with a partner and others in large social groups. It is the same with dance – some people will want to dance on their own; others will want to dance with a partner or a group of friends.

We all have a natural energy – some people rush about all of the time. Some people are very laid back, have a relaxed attitude to life and move in a languid way. Others are natural extroverts with a loud energy that bursts out; others are shy and contained. Most of us are complex beings that do not fit into any single group. However, our temperament, natural energy, fitness, personality and even our taste in music will influence the dance styles that suit us.

The five elements of dance

All styles of dance comprise five elements:

1 **Action**
2 **Body**
3 **Dynamic energies**
4 **Relationship**
5 **Spatial patterns**

Each style combines these elements in different ways. Some styles, such as ballet, are highly stylised with names for each step, established repertoires of work and formalised training programmes. Others remain more informal and improvised, such as belly dancing. It is the way that these elements are combined that gives different styles their particular qualities and feel. Hopefully you will have fun trying all of the styles in this book, but the quick-reference table might help you decide where to begin.

Dance styles: Quick reference table

Style	Fitness level (low, moderate, high)	Complexity level (low, moderate, high)	Key points	Partner	Solo	Individual dances performed in a group
American line dance	Low	Low	Lots of footwork, and changes of direction.		✓	✓
Argentine tango	Moderate	High	Improvised. Subtle communication between partners.	✓		
Ballet	High	High	Turned out legs, strong articulated feet.		✓	
Belly dance	Low	Low/moderate	Improvised. Easy to grasp concepts, but hard to do well.		✓	
Bollywood	High	Low/moderate	Energetic and flamboyant. Upper and lower body moving in different rhythms.		✓	✓
Burlesque	Low	Low	Sassy, lots of posing.		✓	
Flamenco	Moderate	High	Fast and percussive feet movements with lyrical arms and upright posture.		✓	
Tap	Moderate	Moderate	Loose ankles, low centre of gravity and bent knees. Rhythm and timing central.		✓	
Theatre jazz	High	Moderate	Energetic, needing strength and flexibility.		✓	
Waltz	Moderate	Moderate	Graceful and elegant, rise and fall through the feet.	✓		

It's important to remember that although you will find some styles easier than others to master, you may find it difficult to do any of the steps the first time that you try, particularly if you have not danced before. Initially your brain will be confused about what you are asking and it may take a while to co-ordinate and get your body to do what you want it to do and travel in the direction that you want it to go!

Finding a dance class

Once you have found a style (or two) that you want to explore further, a good way to progress is to attend regular classes, or go on a dancing weekend or holiday. Fortunately, as interest in dance has increased in recent years, there are many more opportunities for adults to dance in different styles. However, access can vary in different regions and it can be complicated to understand the qualifications of the teachers leading the classes.

Some useful addresses are detailed for each style explored in this book (see page 194) and these are good places to find out more about qualified teachers offering classes. Many local authorities now include dance classes on their websites and there is an increasing number of directories online focusing on particular dance styles or geographic areas.

Getting started

It is important to take a few minutes before you start dancing to check that both the space where you are going to dance and you yourself are ready. It needn't take long but will keep you safe and make dancing more fun.

Preparing the space

Ideally you will have a clear space with a wooden floor and good ventilation. If you have access to a purpose-built dance studio, congratulations, you are ready to go! For the rest of us, we may be finding the 'best fit' so that we can get started. Don't be afraid to be inventive and remember that different dance styles will require different amounts of space.

HELPFUL HINT
If you are learning with friends, why not share the hire cost of a local hall or suitable room in a local venue?

Simple safety rules

Whatever size space you are using, you need to follow a few simple rules to keep yourself as safe as possible:

- Remove any obstacles that could hurt you if you knocked into them, such as chairs and tables.
- Be aware that tiles are slippery, carpets can burn and rugs are a complete no go – you could trip or slip.
- If you want to use tap shoes, remember they will damage your floor. A couple of pieces of hardboard from your local DIY superstore to cover the area where you are dancing should do the trick.
- Make sure that the room is not too cold, or too hot.
- Ensure that you can easily see this book or screen, if you are using the web links.
- If you are using a mirror (so that you can see the shapes and lines that you are making), check that it is stable and positioned in a safe place.

HELPFUL HINT
Instead of using a mirror, film yourself on your mobile phone to see if you look like the dancer demonstrating, or work with a friend to check each other's positions.

Preparing yourself

Once you have made the room as safe as you can, you need to prepare your body and mind so that you are ready to start dancing. Each dance style has particular shoes and clothing that help you to get the right feel and technique for that style. When you start exploring particular styles in this book, you will find some guidance about what to wear. However, don't worry too much – as long as you wear loose comfortable clothing and some soft-soled, flat shoes (that allow your feet to flex and stretch), or simply bare feet, you will be ready to get started with the warm-ups.

Health and fitness

Dance styles vary in the level of muscle strength, stamina and flexibility needed, so it is important that you are honest with yourself about your level of fitness and general health before you begin to use this book. It is great to use dance as a way to get fit, but start gently and build up gradually. If you are very unfit, just do the warm-up activities until you can do them comfortably. Don't forget to look at the quick reference table on page 13 for a guide about the fitness required and the complexity level of each style. It is very important to consult your doctor before using this book or learning to dance if you:

◆ Are on any medication.
◆ Have recently had surgery.
◆ Have an underlying health condition.
◆ Have an injury, particularly to your knees, back or hips.
◆ Are pregnant.

If in doubt, consult a medical practitioner. You doctor will be able to tell you whether it is safe for you to dance.

HELPFUL HINT
Don't wear jewellery to start with, as it can be a danger and a distraction.

Warming up

This section gives a few warm-up activities to do before you start to dance. There will be additional practice tasks in each of the sections relating to specific dance styles. Warm-up activities are important to get you focused and ready to begin.

Basic alignment

To be able to dance in any style it is important to have good basic alignment of your body. This will allow you to move freely and adapt to the different postures and range of movements needed in the dance styles we are going to explore.

1 Stand in bare feet or flat, soft-soled shoes (they must allow your feet to flex and stretch) with your feet hip-width apart and in parallel, facing straight forward.

2 Be aware of your weight being equally spread across all of your toes, the outer rim of each foot and your heels.

3 Align your body by feeling that your hips are over your knees, your shoulders are over your hips and the weight is passing straight through the centre of your body. Your head should move easily and your chin should be level to the floor.

4 Increase the space between your bottom rib and the top of your pelvis by pulling in your stomach muscles and imagining yourself reaching for the ceiling with your head (most of us can grow a bit!).

5 Your arms should be relaxed and hang loosely at the side of your body. If you have seams down the sides of your trousers your fingers should rest on these.

> **WARNING**
> Before learning any of the dance styles in this book, make sure that you are comfortable doing all of the following exercises at least at the basic level. Dance is about fun, enjoyment and expression, but we need some body strength and co-ordination to be safe.

Basic stance

Most people stand with their feet either turned in (pigeon toed) or turned out (facing away). They need to be facing straight ahead.

pigeon toed

turned out

Parallel

> **HELPFUL HINT**
> Find a line on the floor and use it to help you check that your feet are in parallel.

Three quick tasks to get you started

These tasks will help you with basic body awareness, posture and balance. You would be surprised at how many people find them a challenge! If you do have difficulty with any of these tasks, carry them out alongside the warm-up activities until you can do them easily.

HELPFUL HINT
Be aware of the direction you are facing and where your limbs are as you move about in your daily life. Check they are where you think they should be!

Quick task 1
Body awareness check

Stand facing a mirror, or next to a friend, and lift your arm to the side. Either check in the mirror or ask your friend to check where your arm is.

◆ Most people's arm won't be to the side. If it is, well done – you have good body awareness.

Quick task 2
Shoulder mobility and strength

Stand against a wall and ensure that your shoulder blades remain on the wall as you lift both arms above your head (or as high as you can get them). You should not feel your shoulders rise up.

◆ If you find this difficult, ask a friend to help by resting their hands lightly on your shoulders while you lift your arms up. Every time they feel your shoulders rising you must stop and realign them before continuing.

Quick task 3
Balance

Stand on one leg and count the number of seconds that you can remain there. The aim is to hold it for at least 30 seconds. If you find it easy, repeat the task with your eyes closed.

◆ Remember to try this task on each leg.

HELPFUL HINT
Hold onto the back of a chair until you can hold the position for ten seconds with your eyes open.

Basic alignment and breathing

1 Getting ready to start

- Stand in parallel.
- Put on a piece of your favourite music and shake each part of your body in turn – start with a small movement and then make it bigger and bigger.
- Stop and return to your basic alignment, checking that you are in the correct position.
- Repeat, shaking and stopping until you are slightly out of breath but still in control.
- Enjoy your heart pumping and your muscles relaxing. If you have not moved much recently, take it easy.

WARNING
Stop when you are tired – you don't want to injure yourself before you start!

stand in parallel

Suggested music

If you want to use music, choose anything that you like with a steady 4/4 beat, or use one of the following suggested pieces:

- *The Last Time*, The Rolling Stones
- *Let's Dance*, David Bowie
- *Alfie*, Lily Allen

3 Repeat the breathing exercise using your arms

- As you inhale for five seconds, raise your arms up to the side, palms up.
- As you exhale for five seconds, lower your arms back to their original position, palms down.
- Repeat five times.

TECHNIQUE TIP
Your shoulders should remain at the same level as you lift your arms. Most of us raise our shoulders when we try to lift our arms. Try to keep your shoulders down.

stand in parallel

inhale up

2 Basic alignment and breathing

- Stand in parallel – check your alignment.
- Take a breath in (inhale) for the count of five seconds.
- Let the breath out (exhale) for the count of five seconds.
- Repeat, inhaling and exhaling five times.

TECHNIQUE TIP

Be aware of your breath and alignment. You should be perfectly still, apart from your ribcage expanding to the side as you breathe in and contracting as you breathe out.

stand in parallel

inhale/exhale

exhale down

return to parallel

Walking and transferring weight

1 Walking with toes leading

◆ Stand in parallel.

◆ Stepping on right foot, walk forward down the room with toe leading.

◆ Bring feet together on last step (back to parallel).

> **HELPFUL HINT**
> Don't worry about counts, just notice how the walks feel when you lead with different parts of your feet.

start position

forward right foot lead

forward left foot toe lead

3 Repeat task with heel leading as you walk

◆ Step forward on right foot; heel leading and touching the floor first.

◆ Walk down the room as many times as you can.

◆ Close parallel with last step, ready to start walking backward down the room.

◆ Step backward on right foot, heel leading.

◆ Walk backward down the room with heel leading.

◆ Bring feet to parallel on last step.

start position

forward right foot heel lead

forward left foot heel lead

2 Add walking backward

- ◆ Step backward on right foot, brush top of toes along the floor before stepping onto right foot.
- ◆ Walk backward down the room with toe leading.
- ◆ Bring feet into parallel on last step.

start position   backward right foot toe lead   backward left foot toe lead

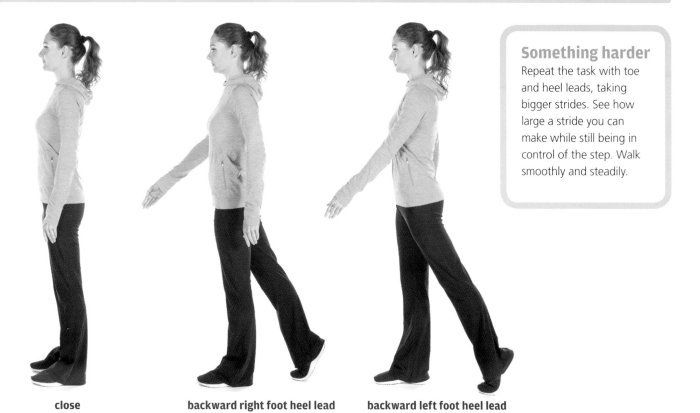

close   backward right foot heel lead   backward left foot heel lead

Something harder

Repeat the task with toe and heel leads, taking bigger strides. See how large a stride you can make while still being in control of the step. Walk smoothly and steadily.

Waist twists

1 Four waist twists right, left, right, left

- ◆ Stand in parallel with arms by side.
- ◆ Twist right, from waist as far as you can without turning hips.
- ◆ Return to centre.
- ◆ Twist left from waist as far as you can without turning hips.
- ◆ Return centre.
- ◆ Repeat four times (right, centre, left, centre, right, centre, left, centre).

TECHNIQUE TIP
Keep a slow steady rhythm as you do this warm-up

start position

waist twist right

2 Add four twists from hips right, left, right, left

- ◆ Twist from hips right, bend knees slightly, let arms swing naturally.
- ◆ Twist from hips left, bend knees slightly, let arms swing naturally.
- ◆ Repeat four times (right, left, right, left).
- ◆ Finish fourth twist in parallel, ready to repeat whole task, turning left first.
- ◆ Repeat whole task four times.

start position

twist right from hips

twist left from hips

x4

centre

waist twist left

centre

Replace the fourth twist with a turn

twist right
from hips

step left foot
to face front

step right foot
to face back

step left foot to face front
ready to start the task again
with a swing to the left side

Articulation of the feet

1 Right foot to ball of foot

- ◆ Stand with feet in parallel, arms by sides.
- ◆ Press right foot into floor so hard that heel comes off floor, toes stay firmly on floor (ball).
- ◆ Lower heel back to floor, press into floor to do this.

HELPFUL HINT
Imagine you are peeling the sole of your foot off the floor. Don't worry about counts, just try to master each stage of the movement.

start position · ball right foot

2 Add a peel of foot from the ball to tip of toe

- ◆ Press right foot into floor so hard that heel comes off floor (as in Step 1).
- ◆ Continue pressing through the ball of right foot until only tip of toe touches floor (tip).
- ◆ Lower heel back to floor, press back through the ball of foot to do this.

HELPFUL HINT
Your hips should remain level and still. Place your hands on your hips while you do the exercise to check that your hips don't move.

start position · ball right foot

3 Add a peel of foot from the ball to the tip of toe and then off the floor

- ◆ Push right foot into the floor so hard that heel comes off the floor.
- ◆ Continue pressing through ball of right foot, through tip of right toe touching floor until all right foot peels just off floor.
- ◆ Return heel to floor, pressing from the tip of toe and through ball to lower heel to floor.

start position · ball right foot

lower heel

HELPFUL HINT

If you find this hard or if it is a new movement for you, hold onto the back of a chair until you master it. This will help your balance.

WARNING

Your feet may ache if you have not done a lot of exercise for a while. This is because you are stretching ligaments and muscles – don't overdo things.

ball right foot

tip right foot

ball right foot

lower heel right foot

tip right foot

off floor right foot

4 Join all stages of task together

- Stand with feet in parallel and arms by sides.
- Right foot ball.
- Right foot heel, lower right foot.
- Right foot ball, right foot tip of toe, lower right foot through ball.
- Right foot ball, right foot tip of toe, right foot off, lower right foot through tip of toe and ball.
- Repeat whole task four times starting with alternate feet (right, left, right, left).

Shoulder mobility

1 Shoulder circle – circle right shoulder backward

- Stand feet in parallel and arms by sides.
- Circle right shoulder backward, making a circle in the joint.

TECHNIQUE TIP
When you have a feel for the movement, add in the counts.

start position

circle right shoulder backwards

2 Add circle right shoulder backward, elbow leading

- Place right hand on right shoulder.
- Circle right shoulder backward with elbow leading; keep hand on shoulder throughout.

HELPFUL HINT
If you find touching your shoulder with your hand difficult, practise doing this before you do the next section.

start position

circle right shoulder backwards, elbow leading

3 Add a full arm circle with right arm

◆ Keep right arm as straight as possible, right to the end of fingers.
◆ Circle right arm backward, passing as close to ear as possible.

4 Join all stages of the task together

◆ Circle right shoulder.
◆ Circle right shoulder, elbow lead.
◆ Circle right arm.
◆ Repeat four times using alternate arms (right, left, right, left).

start position

circle right arm backwards

Something harder
Combine arms and feet

◆ Combine Warm-up task 4 with Warm-up task 5, so that you move your arm and foot at the same time
◆ Stand in parallel with arms by sides.
◆ Circle right shoulder, right foot to ball.
◆ Circle right shoulder, elbow leading, right foot to tip.
◆ Circle right arm, right foot off.
◆ Return to parallel.
◆ Stand still in parallel.
◆ Repeat with left foot and left arm.
◆ Repeat whole task four times.

1 2   3 4   5 6

TECHNIQUE TIP
You have two counts for each move and two counts to check your balance before starting to the other side. This task will test both your balance and co-ordination.

PATTERN FEET	Right foot ball lower heel	Right foot ball, right foot tip toe lower heel	Right foot ball, right foot tip toe, right foot off, lower heel	Still in parallel
PATTERN ARM	Circle right shoulder	Circle right shoulder elbow lead	Circle right arm	Still by side of body
TIMING	**1** 2	3 4	5 6	7 8

Head and neck turns and tilts

1 Head turns right and left

- Stand in parallel, arms relaxed by sides, look straight in front.
- Turn head a ¼ turn right, return to centre.
- Turn head a ¼ turn left, return to centre.
- Repeat to each side (right, centre, left, centre, right, centre, left, centre).

> **WARNING**
> Be careful with your neck. Do not force it further than it can easily turn – treat your neck with care and respect.

¼ turn right
1 2

centre
3 4

¼ turn left
5 6

centre
7 8

Playing with counts

1 Clap a steady rhythm of eight counts

- Stand in parallel, or sit on a chair if more comfortable.
- Clap eight times in a steady beat.

2 Replace claps with stamps, smiles and stillness

- Replace two claps with stamps of feet (i.e. counts 3 and 5).
- Replace another two claps with a gesture (i.e. a smile on count 2 and 6).
- Replace another two claps with silence/stillness (i.e. counts 4 and 7).
- Repeat the phrase. Try it without music and with either a piece of the suggested music (page 18) or a piece of your own choice.

clap
1

smile
2

stamp
3

silence/stillness
4

2 Add head tilts right and left

- ◆ Tilt head right, return to centre.
- ◆ Tilt head left, return to centre.
- ◆ Repeat to each side (right, centre, left, centre, right, centre, left, centre).

TECHNIQUE TIP
Make sure that your ear moves towards your shoulder – do not take your shoulder to your ear!

tilt right　　　　　**centre**　　　　　**tilt left**　　　　　**centre**

HELPFUL HINT
Replace two beats of clapping at a time and practise the sequence of claps and movements until you can remember it, before replacing another two beats.

TECHNIQUE TIP
As you get fitter and stronger, increase the number of repetitions for each exercise. Do this gradually; it is more important to do the exercises accurately than to do lots of repetitions.

stamp　　　　　**smile**　　　　　**silence/stillness**　　　　　**clap**

5　　　　　6　　　　　7　　　　　8

Cooling down

When you finish dancing, it is always important to cool your body down and stretch out your muscles. The more energetic the dance that you are doing, the more important it is that you cool down properly.

Always remember when you stop dancing to do at least two of the cool-down activities. This will get you into the habit of cooling down at the end of your dancing and returning your blood flow to normal.

Returning to everyday life

Walk briskly around your house, entering every room at least once. Keep walking gradually moving more slowly for at least three minutes and then do at least two small household chores, such as tidying some things away, washing some dishes or loading/unloading the dishwasher.

inhale up

exhale down

Breathing with arms

◆ Stand in parallel, arms by sides. Feel the same alignment as at the start of the warm-ups.

◆ Inhale for four counts, raise arms up to the side, palms up.

◆ Exhale for four counts, lower arms back to original position, palms down.

Leg stretches

1 Hamstring stretch

- Stand in parallel, holding the chair:
- Place left foot forward. Keep right leg straight, foot flat on floor.
- Slowly bend left knee, transferring weight over left foot until you feel a stretch in right leg.
- Hold position for 15 seconds.
- Repeat placing right foot forward.

TECHNIQUE TIP

Don't worry if you can't hold the stretch for the full 15 seconds when you start. You will work up to this the more that you do the exercises.

hold chair left foot forward

transfer weight

2 Glute stretch

- Stand in parallel, holding the chair, knees slightly flexed.
- Keep knees flexed and together.
- Lift right leg, behind, bent at knee joint.
- Reach right arm behind, hold right foot.
- Slowly and gently pull right toe towards your bottom until you feel a stretch in the front thigh.
- Hold position for 15 seconds.
- Repeat lifting left leg.

hold chair

lift right leg and gently pull towards bottom

Cool-down task 2
Tricep stretches

1 Stretch, holding on to your elbow

- Stand in parallel.
- Lift right arm overhead (or as high as you can get it) bent at elbow joint, so the palm of hand touches your back and fingers face towards floor.
- Place left arm overhead, to reach right elbow, slowly and gently pull elbow so you feel a gentle stretch in right arm.
- Hold for 15 seconds.
- Repeat using left arm.

stand in parallel

right elbow up

Cool-down task 3
Back curls

1 Curl at the top of back

- Stand in parallel.
- Starting with head, imagine moving one vertebra at a time to roll down your spine so that the top of your back is curled.
- Check your alignment is correct and your breathing calm and steady.
- Repeat twice.

GET STARTED
You are now ready to start exploring some of the dance styles in this book. Remember to be honest about your fitness and general health level when choosing where to begin.

WARNING
Move slowly and gradually, do not rush or roll too far.

stand in parallel

head forward

32 Dance Manual ◆ **Cooling down**

2 Add taking right arm across chest, as close to body and as straight as possible

- ◆ Hold right arm with left arm, just above or below, elbow joint.
- ◆ Slowly and gently pull right arm closer to body.
- ◆ Hold the position for 15 seconds.
- ◆ Repeat using left arm.

TECHNIQUE TIP
Do not twist your upper body or let your shoulder fall forward when you do this.

stand in parallel

right arm across, hold with left arm

shoulders forward

shoulders return

head return

Tap dance

Tap dance is an enduring favourite with both men and women who want to dance. It attracts followers from a large age range and a small number of steps performed very quickly always makes a big impression.

It has developed into two distinct styles:

1 **Broadway tap (tapping)** combines the percussive footwork with other dance styles, such as ballet and jazz.

2 **Rhythm tap (hoofing)** works more closely with different rhythms, using the heels, toes and many other parts of the shoe to make sounds.

Hoofing is often improvised and is more relaxed than the theatrical and flamboyant Broadway tap.

As with many styles of dance, it is difficult to know the precise origins of tap. It is generally accepted, however, that in the 1800s, immigrants from England, Ireland and Scotland brought their clog dance heritage with a bit of hornpipe and jig to America. Over time in the clubs, dancers blended these foot movements with the drumming rhythms used by African Americans.

William Henry Lane, known as Master Juba is often credited as being the first tapper and by 1845 was a famous performer in Minstrel shows. Dancers such as Bill 'Bojangles' Robinson continued to develop and shape tap dancing towards the technique recognised today. He started performing as a child in 1884, making the transition to Vaudeville variety shows that provided a glorious platform for tap dancers. Tap acts were extremely popular with audiences and therefore competition to get bookings was tough, so performers needed to find a way to stand out and be noticed. To do this, they started blending tap with other dance styles, acrobatics and props to create their own personal style. Many Vaudeville performers were family acts, including such stars as Fred Astaire who danced with his sister Adele, and Gene Kelly who performed with his four siblings.

The explosion in popularity of the Hollywood Musical in the 1930s and 1940s fed the enthusiasm for tap dancing. The skills of tap dancers – such as Gene Kelly, who combined tap with athleticism and grace, and Fred Astaire who, along with Ginger Rogers gave tap and ballroom a legendary twist – were ideal for the 'feel good' stories.

Tap fell out of favour as the enthusiasm for musicals fell; however, the 1980s saw a revival helped by Gregory Hines, who starred in *White Nights* with Mikhail Baryshnikov (1985) and *Tap* (1989).

In the 1990s, Adam Garcia, best known as a judge on *Got to Dance*, co-founded a group that thrust tap back into the spotlight when it evolved into the Australian group Tap Dogs. The mix of high-energy physical tap dancing performed by dancers dressed as builders and a set designed as a construction site was an instant hit. *Tap Dogs* is now a West End show and demand for their tours remains high across the world.

The most important part of tap is the sound, and therefore the shoe. Initially, sounds were made by wooden-soled shoes used in clog dancing, followed by experiments with leather shoes and adding coins or hobnails in the soles. Thomas Rice is often credited with inventing the tap shoe when he added metallic soles to his shoes in 1882 to add sound to the movements, but no one really knows if this is true!

Tap dance and music

Tap has a strong relationship with music, although it is less about moving to music as becoming part of the music. It is important that the dancer keeps a steady beat with their taps so that they can then play with the accents and counts within the music.

Broadway musicals saw the arrival of lighter leather shoes with metal taps on the toes and sometimes heels as well. Tap shoes make three different types of taps – teletone, duotone and supertone. The difference in tone depends on the number and position of the screws keeping 'the tap' in place on the bottom of the shoe. Experienced tap dancers often loosen or tighten their 'taps' to gain a more hollow or crisper tap sound to suit their style.

The names of the steps vary from country to country and sometimes from region to region, but people usually perform similar steps playing with the rhythm of the music and bringing in elements of their own personalities and dance experiences.

The tap class

Adult tap dance classes are always very popular and last for about an hour. Many classes in the UK and America offer a blend of different tap styles. Class members usually stand in lines behind the teacher and begin with a warm-up to stretch their muscles, particularly those in their legs and feet.

The next section of the class will include tasks and sequences, practising steps that class members already know and learning new ones. Classes usually finish with a group dance that is built up over a number of weeks, so everyone gets a sense of performing alongside learning the steps. The teacher will always lead a cool-down before the class ends.

Many adult classes do not follow a formal syllabus, but examination boards such as The Imperial Society of Teachers of Dancing (ISTD) have developed syllabi for adult tap and examinations, which some teachers do follow. Teachers are usually relaxed about whether class members take examinations; it's more an opportunity for those that want to rather than a must.

Dress code

Adult tap classes usually have a fairly relaxed dress code, as long as class members are safe and can move easily. The key part is to have the correct footwear; it is difficult to tap dance without tap shoes because you cannot produce the correct sounds. If you are not sure that tap is the dance style for you, wear a formal shoe with a smooth flat sole and low heel for the first few lessons. Never wear trainers or any rubber-soled shoes, sandals, or shoes with platforms or wedge heels, as this will be very frustrating and make dancing unsafe and difficult for you.

As you improve, you will want to buy specialist shoes and these must fit well. Different designs and manufacturers suit different feet, so ask for advice when you are ready to buy a pair and/or try on a range of styles before you finally decide what to buy. Class teachers will often help you find a pair of shoes to suit your feet, as well as your budget.

Starting out

Female
A pair of leggings and a top, or everyday clothing that isn't too tight or too long. Long trousers will get in the way when you are tap dancing, so make sure that they end above your ankle. It's a good idea to tie your hair back if it's long so that it's out of the way. Tap shoes are essential (after the first few lessons) and are usually black. Mary Jane, which has a bar and a low heel, is ideal for beginners, or some people prefer the Oxford – a laced shoe with a broad heel.

Male
Closely fitted T-shirt with shorts or trousers. Long trousers will get in the way when you are tap dancing so make sure that they end above your ankle. The Oxford shoe is a good starter for men.

Stepping up

Male and female
The basic clothing doesn't change, but as you progress you may want to invest in different shoes, or try different tones. Remember you can loosen or tighten the taps to change the sound.

Essential information

1 The posture requires a low centre of gravity; keep your weight slightly forward, knees bent and a relaxed stance with your feet under your body. Try lifting your heels off and balancing on the balls of your feet, without raising your body. You will need to engage your core/tummy muscles to do this.

2 Tap dancing is all about the rhythm and sound. It is important to keep an even beat with your taps so keep your movements large and slow when you start; you can make them smaller and speed up once you have the basic patterns.

3 Tasks are performed starting with the right foot and then repeated starting with the left foot to ensure that the body is worked evenly.

WARNING
Be particularly careful with your knees. If you haven't done much exercise for a while you may feel some soreness in your thighs and ankles.

4 Strong, flexible ankles are important to articulate clear sharp sounds. Try writing the alphabet in the air, one letter at a time, with each foot in turn (make sure that you move from your ankle – your knee and thigh should not move). Sit on a hard chair with your back straight – don't slouch!

Heels and toes

1 Start with the heels

◆ Stand with feet hip-width apart, keep weight forward, knees bent, loose and relaxed with feet under your body.
◆ Lift right heel, place down strongly, hitting heel tap clearly on floor, put weight on whole foot (Heel).
◆ Heel left foot.

Repeat eight times								
PATTERN	Right	Left	Right	Left	Right	Left	Right	Left
TIMING	**1** 2	3 4	5 6	7 8	**2** 2	3 4	5 6	7 8

Suggested music

Anything with a strong steady beat is fine. Remember to choose a slow piece to start, or use a steady drumbeat at a speed that suits you.

◆ *Venus in Furs*, Velvet Underground
◆ *The Lunatics (Have Taken Over The Asylum)*, Fun Boy Three
◆ *2 Hearts*, Kylie Minogue

start position

right heel up

1

right heel down

2

Something harder
Heels and finger click

◆ Stand with feet hip-width apart, keep weight forward, knees bent, loose and relaxed with feet under body.
◆ Heel right foot.
◆ Heel left foot.
◆ Heel right foot (you will have done the movement three times in total).
◆ Click right fingers once.
◆ Repeat the pattern starting with left foot, clicking left fingers.

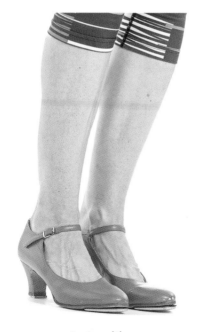

start position

Repeat								
PATTERN	Right	Left	Right	Click	Left	Right	Left	Click
TIMING	**1** 2	3 4	5 6	7 8	**2** 2	3 4	5 6	7 8

2 Add toes

- ◆ You will need to shift your weight slightly backwards.
- ◆ Lift right toe, place down strongly, hitting toe tap clearly on floor, put weight fully on right foot (toe).
- ◆ Toe left foot.
- ◆ Repeat whole task twice.

Repeat eight times								
PATTERN	Right	Left	Right	Left	Right	Left	Right	Left
TIMING	**3** 2	3 4	5 6	7 8	**4** 2	3 4	5 6	7 8

Remember

- ◆ Do the general warm-ups before tackling this section.
- ◆ Practise each section of the tasks separately before joining it onto another section.
- ◆ Repeat the whole task several times when you have joined all of the sections together.

start position

right toe up

1

right toe down

2

right heel up

1

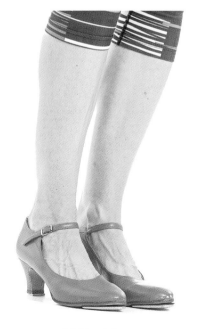

right heel down

2

HELPFUL HINT
If you can't click your fingers, clap your hands or gently tap your thigh instead.

click right fingers

7 8

Practice task 2
Brushes and stamp

1 Forward brush

- Stand with feet hip-width apart, knees bent, relaxed and loose, weight slightly forward.
- Lift right leg, from knee to back and swing right foot forward, so the ball quickly brushes against floor on toe plate of shoe (forward brush).
- Your heel MUST NOT touch the floor, finish with right foot off floor.

TECHNIQUE TIP
Point foot slightly as right leg passes left leg to get a clear tap.

start position

lift right leg from knee to back

brush ball of right foot to finish front

Complete pattern including stamp

- Firmly place right foot flat on floor, put weight on it (stamp).
- Stay still for one count.
- Repeat pattern starting with left foot.

TECHNIQUE TIP
You should only hear one strong sound when you stamp. Two sounds means either your heel or your toe is hitting the floor first.

start position

brush right foot forward

Repeat four times								
PATTERN	Right forward	Right backward	Stamp	Still	Left forward	Left backward	Stamp	Still
TIMING	& 1	& 2	3	4	& 5	& 6	7	8

2 Add a backward brush

◆ Brush right foot backward bending at knee, hitting floor with centre of ball tap of shoe as it passes left leg (brush back).

◆ Finish with right leg lifted from knee behind.

start right foot front

brush ball of right foot finish back

brush right foot backward

stamp right foot

stay still

x4

Tap sequence

Watch the video
Haynes.com/dancemanual

1 Four toe stamps travelling down the room

◆ Stand with feet hip-width apart, knees bent, relaxed and loose, weight slightly forward, with arms down at side. Face front of room.

◆ Place right heel forward, lower toes, transfer weight onto foot.

◆ Place left heel forward, lower toes, transfer weight.

◆ Repeat right, left.

◆ Let arms move naturally (as if walking).

TECHNIQUE TIP
Notice how similar this is to the toe and heel struts in American Line dance.

start position | right foot toe
1

right foot stamp
2

PATTERN	Right	Left	Right	Left
TIMING	**1** 2	3 4	5 6	7 8

2 Add stamp, stamp, step back, step back

◆ Stamp right foot, moving forward.

◆ Stamp left foot, bring left foot parallel with right foot.

◆ Step back on ball of right foot, transfer weight onto right foot.

◆ Step back on ball of left foot, bring left foot parallel with right foot, weight slightly more on left foot.

◆ Repeat making a ¼ turn to right on first stamp, complete stamps and steps facing right side of the room.

stamp right foot
2

stamp left foot
2

stamp back right foot
3

3 Add two shuffle hop steps

- ◆ Brush forward and backward right foot (shuffle).
- ◆ Take off from ball of left foot and land on ball of left foot (hop).
- ◆ Step on ball of right foot, transfer weight onto right foot (step).
- ◆ Repeat shuffle hop step with left foot.

TECHNIQUE TIP
Take one count for every action, keeping an even rhythm.

shuffle right foot
3 2

hop left foot
3

step right foot
4

PATTERN	Shuffle hop step right foot	Shuffle hop step left foot
TIMING	**3** 2 3 4	5 6 7 8

step back left foot
4

repeat making ¼ turn right on right foot stamp
5 6 7 8

Suggested music

- ◆ *These Boots Are Made For Walkin'*, Nancy Sinatra
- ◆ *Singin' In The Rain*, Gene Kelly.

Tap sequence *continued*

4 **Add three stamp and brushes and two stamps, making a curved pathway to finish facing front**

- ◆ Stamp right foot, forward brush left foot.
- ◆ Stamp left foot, forward brush right foot.
- ◆ Stamp right foot, forward brush left foot.
- ◆ Stamp left foot, close right foot to left foot with a stamp, finish facing front ready to repeat whole sequence starting with left foot.

stamp right foot
4

forward brush left foot
2

stamp left foot
3

forward brush right foot
4

Something harder
Play with the timing

- ◆ Do four shuffle hop steps in the same time as the two in the original sequence.
- ◆ Include pick up steps in the stamp and step back section (this gives an extra sound in the movement).
- ◆ Stamp right foot, moving forward.
- ◆ Stamp left foot, bring left foot parallel with right foot.
- ◆ Lift right toe and pull it back, hitting toe tap on floor BEFORE stepping back on right foot (pick up). Remember to step onto the ball of foot and transfer weight.
- ◆ Pick up left foot. Remember to step back parallel with your right foot.
- ◆ Repeat making a 1/4 turn right on right foot stamp.

HELPFUL HINT
Practise the pickups separately before putting into the sequence.

lift right toe

HELPFUL HINT
Turn slightly every time you stamp so that you end up facing the front of the room for your last stamp (count 7).

stamp right foot

5

forward brush left foot

6

stamp left foot

7

stamp right foot

8

pull right toe back hitting tap on floor

&

step back right foot

3

pick up step left foot

& 4

The waltz

The waltz is an enduring favourite of the dance floor; it is the dance that features in fairy tales and is traditionally the first dance at weddings.

Television programmes such as *Strictly Come Dancing* in the UK and *Dancing with the Stars* in America have helped a new generation to fall in love with the waltz. It remains the byword for grace and elegance, and is also much harder than it looks!There are three key types of waltz:

1   The Viennese waltz
2   The Old Time waltz
3   The Modern waltz

The Viennese waltz originated in Vienna in the 18th century and has roots in early Austrian and Bavarian folk dances, such as the Ländler. When it arrived in the UK in the early 19th century, via the Parisian courts, it was considered quite scandalous due to the closeness of the embrace. The tempo for the Viennese waltz is almost twice as fast as for the Modern waltz. The dancers never stop turning, first one way and then the other, always moving anti-clockwise around the room.

The Old Time waltz was based on the five positions of ballet and it was an art to be able to gain the fluidity of movement. It remained popular for many years, but has gradually given way to the Modern waltz.

The Modern waltz is sometimes referred to by several other names, including the Slow waltz (because it has a slower tempo than the Viennese waltz), the Diagonal waltz (as this is the direction a couple faces to start the dance) and the English waltz (as it is called in mainland Europe).

The Modern waltz arose out of the period of political and social change between the two world wars. In 1919 the zest for life immediately following the end of the First World War alongside Ragtime music, which had arrived from America, combined to bring greater freedom and improvisation on the dance floor that spilled over into ballroom dances.

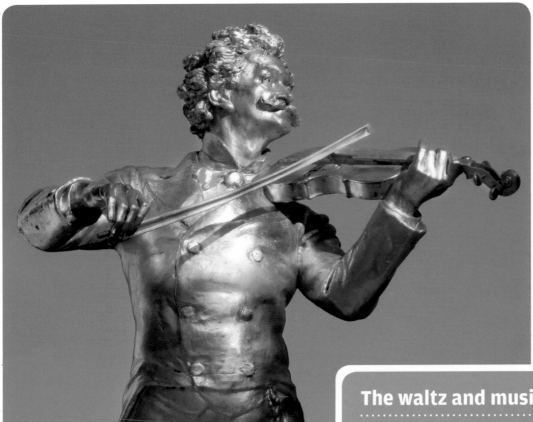

In 1929 The Official Board of Ballroom Dancing (OBBD), now known as The British Dance Council (BDC), was created to standardise several ballroom dances including the waltz, setting strict tempos and regulating the steps to regain some control over what was happening on the dance floor.

The Modern waltz includes swinging, swaying and accented rises. It famously needs dancers to lead from the heel and when done properly creates the feel of gliding across the floor.

Vernon and Irene Castle are often credited with making the waltz popular and accessible, hosting tea dances and appearing on Broadway in shows such as *Lady of the Slipper* (1912) and *Sunshine Girl* (1913). They starred in silent movies including *The Whirl of Life* (1915), which was based on their lives and confirmed their status as a celebrity couple. In 1914, they famously undertook a tour of America and Europe, visiting 32 cities in 28 days – an amazing feat considering the transport infrastructure in that era.

Victor Silvester was World Ballroom Dance Champion in 1922. He is better known for his big band sounds and for being the first person to provide music at a strict tempo for each of the ballroom dances, including the waltz. Standardising the music meant that wherever people danced the waltz, the tempo of the music would be the same. It also meant that Victor Silvester became very famous, selling lots

The waltz and music

The 3/4 time signature of the waltz gives a distinctive feel to the dance. Joseph Lanner, Johann Strauss, his son Johann Straus II and Schubert are some of the greatest composers associated with the waltz, and its popularity in the 19th century was partly due to their music.

From the 1930s, Victor Silvester led the way for arranging popular music to strict tempo for the modern waltz (84–90 beats per minute). This continues today, with musicians taking new releases and arranging them to a strict modern waltz tempo. Maestro records are still a key producer and supplier of strict tempo music for the waltz and other ballroom and Latin dances.

of records, having his own long-running radio programme and appearing on television. Other orchestras and big bands followed – Tony Evans and the Blackpool Tower Orchestra are two of the most well known.

The rules for waltzing on the dance floor

1 All couples move in an anticlockwise direction.
2 The man, or leader, starts with the wall nearest his right arm.
3 The waltz starts with the man facing diagonally towards the wall, down the Line of Dance (the direction that the couple will move).

The waltz class

Classes last for about an hour and the teacher will usually start the class by teaching some steps or a collection of steps (figure). He or she will then circulate, giving advice and dancing with different pairs as they practise the figures.

In the UK, people usually attend classes with a partner. If you attend on your own the teacher will run the class so that you can be involved, but in reality you will not get as much out of the class, so take a friend with you, even if you swap between leader and follower roles.

Many classes work towards medals, although it is not obligatory for you to do so. The Imperial Society of Teachers of Dancing (ISTD) and the International Dance Teachers' Association (IDTA) are two leading bodies for ballroom dance in the UK and most teachers will have qualifications from one of these boards.

Teachers often hold social events in the form of tea dances or evening dances, where people come and undertake various ballroom and Latin dances. These events encourage camaraderie among those attending classes and give new starters a chance to see more experienced dancers in action and to dance alongside them. If you are a new

starter, don't worry about getting in the way of a more experienced couple on the dance floor – it is their responsibility to give way to you! Social events are a great chance to dress up and practise dancing, and although recorded music is often used, live music is sometimes provided by a keyboard player.

Dress code

Most classes are informal and people wear styles that they like and that suit them. The key is to have appropriate footwear. Neither men nor women need to invest in ballroom shoes for the first lesson, but it is important to have shoes that support your ankles and do not stick to the floor. Never wear trainers or any rubber-soled shoes, sandals, or shoes with platforms or wedge heels, as this will be very frustrating and make dancing difficult and unsafe for you.

As you improve you will want to buy specialist shoes. These must fit well. Different designs and manufacturers suit different feet, so ask for advice when you are ready to buy a pair and/or try on a range of styles before you finally decide what to buy. Class teachers will often help you find a pair of shoes that suit your feet as well as your budget.

Starting out

Female

It's best to wear skirts and dresses as they help get the feel of the movement although any comfortable lightweight clothing that doesn't restrict your movement is fine. A 'Sunday shoe', such as a court shoe with a small heel, is ideal. The heel will help you to achieve the correct stance, but it must be at a height that you are used to wearing.

Male

Lightweight, comfortable trousers and a shirt or T-shirt are ideal at first. Light shoes with a thin, flexible sole are ideal, or an everyday shoe without a hard sole will get you started.

Stepping up

Female

As you progress you will want to invest in a pair of specialist ballroom shoes. You may want to buy a 'Practice Dress', which is fitted and made of soft fabrics to show the line and shapes that you are making when you dance.

Male

Again, you will want to invest in a pair of specialist ballroom shoes. You may also want to buy specialist trousers and fitted shirts that give a better line when you dance.

Essential information

1 The frame is key to waltzing successfully: stand so that right sides of leader and follower bodies touch. Leader cups follower's shoulder blade. *(Follower place left hand on leader's upper arm.)* Angle your head diagonally left, between your partner's right ear and your own left hand.

2 Both partners need equal tension in their arms to hold the frame. Get a feel for this by walking with your partner in a simple double-arm hold.

3 Tilt your pelvis slightly forward (this makes it feel as if your bottom is sticking out). Lift up from your pelvis through your ribcage – not your shoulders!

4 Your feet should never leave the floor – this gives the gliding feel of the waltz.

REMEMBER
Personal hygiene is particularly important when dancing with a partner.

The change step

1 Left foot change step

- ◆ Stand, by yourself, with feet together, arms naturally at side.
- ◆ Step forward left foot, transfer weight over foot.
- ◆ Step side right foot, transfer weight over foot.
- ◆ Close left foot to right foot, transfer weight over left foot releasing right foot to start the next change step.

start position	**step forward left foot**	**step side right foot**	**close left foot to right foot**
	1	2	3

3 Add backward left foot and backward right foot change step

- ◆ Step backward left foot, transfer weight over foot.
- ◆ Step side right foot, transfer weight over foot.
- ◆ Close left foot to right foot, transfer weight over left foot releasing right foot to start next change step.
- ◆ Step backward right foot, transfer weight over foot.
- ◆ Step side left foot, transfer weight over foot.
- ◆ Close right foot to left foot, transfer weight over right foot releasing left foot to start the next step.

HELPFUL HINT
To get the feel of the movement, keep repeating the left foot and right foot change steps as many times as you can moving around the room.

start position	**step backwards left foot**	**step side right foot**	**close left foot to right foot**
	3	2	3

2 Add a right foot change step

- ◆ Step forward right foot, transfer weight over foot.
- ◆ Step side left foot, transfer weight over foot.
- ◆ Close right foot to left foot, transfer weight over right foot releasing left foot to start the next change step.

Remember
....

- ◆ Warm up before tackling this section.
- ◆ Practise each section of the tasks separately before joining it onto another section.
- ◆ Repeat the whole task several times when you have joined all of the sections together.
- ◆ Refresh your memory of the abbreviations by looking at the introduction again.

start position

step forward right foot

2

step side left foot

2

close right foot to left foot

3

HELPFUL HINT
Holding onto your tummy muscles makes this easier

Repeat the task with some rise and fall

- ◆ Step side onto ball of foot.
- ◆ Rise to your toes as you close your feet together

step backwards right foot

4

step side left foot

2

close right foot to left foot

3

Forward change steps with partner

1 Get into ballroom hold

- Leader face where you are going to dance (Line of Dance). *(Follower face the leader arms-length away.)*
- Leader takes follower's right hand in their left hand, draws follower towards them, slightly off centre, so that both partner's right sides are touching.
- Both look left.
- Leader cups follower's shoulder blade. *(Follower place left hand on leader's upper arm.)*

HELPFUL HINT
Traditionally, only the leader's steps are given, but in this book the follower's steps are in green italics.

2 Add a left foot change step

- Leader step forward on left foot. *(Follower step backward on right foot.)*
- Leader step side onto ball of right foot. *(Follower step side onto ball of left foot.)*
- Leader close left foot to right foot rising to toe on both feet. *(Follower close right foot to left foot rising to toes on both.)*

HELPFUL HINT
Your weight should always be more over one foot or the other. NEVER split your weight equally between both feet.

3 Add a right foot change step:

- Leader step forward right foot. *(Follower step backward left foot.)*
- Leader step side onto ball of left foot. *(Follower step side onto ball of right foot.)*
- Leader close right foot to left foot rising to toes on both feet. *(Follower close left foot to right foot rising to toes on both feet.)*
- Repeat left foot and right foot, change steps as many times as you can.

HELPFUL HINT
Closing the feet is important. Think of bringing your ankles together and your feet will have to follow.

step forward right foot
step backward left foot
2

step side left foot
step side right foot
2

step forward left foot

step backwards right foot

1

step side right foot

step side left foot

2

close left foot to right foot

close right foot to left foot

3

close right foot to left foot

close left foot to right foot

3

Something harder
Work on technique

- ◆ Emphasise the first step and take a smaller step to side.
- ◆ Work on getting the gradual rise onto the toes and lowering of the heels as you do the steps (rise and fall) characteristic of the waltz.
- ◆ Keep your head looking left.

Waltz sequence

Watch the video
Haynes.com/dancemanual

1 Ballroom hold and left foot change step

◆ Get into ballroom hold, Leader facing the Line of Dance (LOD) feet facing 8 o'clock.

◆ Make a left foot change step.

step forward left foot	**step side right foot**	**close left foot to right foot**
step backwards right foot	*step side left foot*	*close right foot to left foot*
1	2	3

2 Add a natural turn

◆ Leader step forward right foot.
(*Follower step backward left foot.*)

◆ Leader step side left foot, making a turn to right.
(*Follower step side right foot, making a turn.*)

◆ Leader close right foot to left foot, end back like of dance feet facing 12 noon. (*Follower close right foot to left foot completing turn, end facing partner.*)

◆ Leader step backward left foot.
(*Follower step forward right foot.*)

◆ Leader step side right foot making a turn to right.
(*Follower step side left foot making a turn.*)

◆ Leader close left foot to right foot, end facing diagonally centre feet facing just before 4 o'clock.
(*Follower close right foot to left foot end facing partner.*)

end of left foot change step

step forward right foot
step backward left foot
2

step side left foot
step side right foot
2

HELPFUL HINT
To get into position on a dance floor to start a waltz, the leader stands diagonally to the wall nearest their right arm.

TECHNIQUE TIP
The leader will start facing diagonally towards the wall and end the natural turn facing diagonally towards the centre of the room.

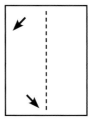

close right to left foot
close left to right foot
3

step backward left foot
step forward right foot
3

step side right foot
step side
2

close left foot to right foot
close right foot to left foot
3

Waltz sequence *continued*

3 Add a right foot change step

◆ Leader strong step forward on right foot.
(Follower step backward on left foot, heel lead.)

◆ Leader step side left foot.
(Follower step side right foot.)

◆ Leader close right foot to left foot.
(Follower close left foot to right foot.)

step backwards left foot
step forwards right foot
4

step side right foot
step side left foot
2

close left foot to right foot
close right foot to left foot
3

4 Add a reverse turn

◆ Leader step forward left foot.
(Follower step backward right foot.)

◆ Leader step to side right foot making a turn to left.
(Follower step to side left foot making a turn.)

◆ Leader close left foot to right foot, back in LOD feet facing 12 noon.
(Follower close right foot to left foot completing turn, end facing front of the room.)

◆ Leader steps backward right foot.
(Follower step forward left foot.)

◆ Leader step side left foot making a turn to left.
(Follower step side right foot making a turn.)

◆ Leader close right foot to left foot, end facing diagonal wall feet facing 8 o'clock.
(Follower close left foot to right foot end facing left corner, back of room.)

end of right foot change step

step forward left foot
step backward right foot
5

step side right foot
step side left foot
2

TECHNIQUE TIP
When turning or rotating, the partner on the inside needs to take smaller steps.

close left foot to right foot
close right foot to left foot
3

step backward right foot
step forward left foot
6

step side left foot
step side right foot
2

close right foot to left foot
close left foot to right foot
3

Something Harder
Introduce a whisk and a chassé

1 Start with a whisk

- Replace the left foot change step at the start of the sequence with a whisk and chassé from promenade position.
- Stand in ballroom hold, diagonally to the wall nearest the leader's right arm.
- Leader step forward left foot. *(Follower step backward right foot.)*
- Leader step side right foot and slightly forward. *(Follower step side left foot.)*
- Leader crosses left foot behind right foot, on toes opening partner into promenade postion. *(Follower crosses right foot behind left foot, turning into promenade position.)*

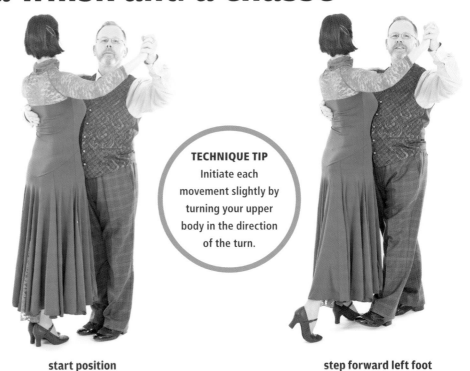

TECHNIQUE TIP
Initiate each movement slightly by turning your upper body in the direction of the turn.

start position
start position

step forward left foot
step backward right foot
1

2 Add a chassé

- Leader step forward right foot, crossing in front of left foot in promenade position. *(Follower step forward left foot, crossing in front of right foot in promenade position.)*
- Leader step side and slightly forward left foot. *(Follower step side right foot, starting to turn to face partner.)*
- Leader close right foot to left foot. *(Follower close left foot to right foot, facing partner.)*
- Leader step side and slightly forward left foot. *(Follower step side and slightly backward right foot.)*
- Finish in the direction of the following step, leader's feet facing 8 o'clock.

step forward right foot in promenade position
step forward left foot in promenade position
2

step side, slightly forward left foot
step side right foot
2

TECHNIQUE TIP
Promenade Position is when the leader's right side and follower's left side are in contact so their bodies make a 'v' position.

step side right foot
step side left foot
2

cross left foot behind right foot into promenade position
cross right foot behind left foot into promenade position
3

3 Continue the sequence from the natural turn

◆ To do this with ease the leader will need to step outside of their partner (on their right side) after the chassé.

close right foot to left foot
close left foot to right foot
&

step side, slightly forward left foot
step side right foot
3

American line dance

The 1990s saw a huge increase in the popularity of American line dancing and it seemed that every town and village across the UK had classes. Although it is no longer so popular, it retains a steady following and classes are widespread in the UK, Europe and America.

As with most dance styles, it is hard to say definitively how line dancing developed. According to folklore, cowboys liked to dance at social events, but this does not mean that they necessarily invented the style, as is often stated. We do know that it has connections with traditional folk dances from Europe and the UK, brought by the first settlers, and American barn and square dances that evolved in the west and mid-west of America in the 1800s. Line dancing today, however, owes more to the 1960s American Soul scene, the love of dancing in lines at discos during the 1970s and – you may be surprised to know – films such as *Saturday Night Fever* (1977) and *Urban Cowboy* (1980).

Before line dances had set choreography, 'callers' moved from town to town calling out the steps for dances as they happened. At large social dances, callers are sometimes still used so that people who don't know the dances can join in. Typically, at large social events in America, bands played at the front of the hall and those who wanted to dance did so at the back of the room. Couples danced around the outside and singles danced in lines in the middle. Space was limited so the dance steps were small, neat and rhythmic. The UK's love for American line dance really took off when the video for Billy Ray Cyrus's recording of *Achy Breaky Heart* (1992) included a mass line dance. Easy choreographed dances such as *Waltz Across Texas* and *Electric Slide* cemented its popularity.

Line dancing is predominantly an individual dance style (although some dances are choreographed for partners). Men and women stand together, face the same direction and dance the same steps at the same time. The cowboy image and the club environment in which classes were originally taught meant that it was a dance form that attracted many men to classes during the 1990s. Cowboy boots and Stetsons were a must for all male dancers and elaborate skirts and

fringed jacket costumes developed for women. The cowboy theme is less prevalent in the UK now, although it remains strong in the USA.

Almost all dances include a change of direction and are known as one-wall, two-wall or four-wall dances. The sequence is the set of dance steps that make up the dance. A dance is made by completing the set sequence a number of times.

◆ One-wall dances face the same direction at the start and end of the sequence.
◆ Two-wall dances face the opposite wall at the end of the sequence.
◆ Four-wall dances have a quarter turn to face the left or right at the end of the sequence.

Don't be fooled into thinking that a one-wall dance will not include any turns; it just means that the sequence finishes back where it started.

Line dance and music

Line dancing is usually performed to recorded music from a broad range of genres, not just country and western music. The steps work clearly with the rhythm and can sometimes have the feel of a particular dance style such as the waltz, salsa or tango.

Dances are always choreographed, sometimes to a particular piece of music, but more typically they work on a 16- (simplest), 32- (general and improver level) or 64- (complex) count sequence that can be performed to many pieces of music. Occasionally, a 96-count sequence is created, although this is not for the faint-hearted! The choreographed dances are easily available to line-dance teachers and as such the same dances are done at all classes, no matter where they are held. So if you are on holiday, you can easily attend a local class and will know at least some of the dances.

The American line dance class

Line dances usually last about an hour. The classes generally start with a gentle, simple line dance known by everyone to get the body and mind warmed up and ready for the class. The teacher usually acts as a caller, demonstrating and calling the dance at the front of the class.

New dances are produced all the time and the teacher will often introduce a new dance during a lesson. If the teacher introduces a new dance, they will teach it slowly without the music and move to the new front of the class (in 2-wall and 4-wall dances) each time the sequence is repeated. Some teachers also take requests for favourite dances, which they then include in the lesson.

It is acceptable for you to sit out of some dances, especially if you are new to a class and haven't danced much before. The hardest and most energetic dances will be done in the middle part of the class. The last dance or two will be slower and easier – this will act as a cool-down before the class finishes.

Classes are generally friendly and a great way to meet new people and get fitter. Class members make space for new people to stand in the middle of a line so that you have someone to follow whichever direction you are

facing. Standing in the back row is not a good idea in a line dance class!

Some classes give the option of taking medal examinations or have a group of people who perform at local events. Companies also run special American line dancing holidays, so if you get really keen, there are lots of ways to develop your skills and get more involved.

Dress code

The dress code generally is anything casual and comfortable although denim jeans remain a favourite with many people. Some groups still keep to the cowboy and cowgirl idea but less so in the UK. It is important to have shoes that do not stick to the floor and have a small heel to help with the turns and 'swivel' needed for the style. Never wear trainers or any rubber-soled shoes, sandals, or shoes with platforms or wedge heels, as this will be very frustrating and make dancing difficult and unsafe for you. Boots are great, as they support your ankles.

Starting out

Female
Wear casual lightweight clothing, either trousers or a full skirt and top. Leather-soled boots or shoes with a low heel are great to get you started.

Male
Casual clothes, such as jeans or lightweight trousers and a shirt or T-shirt, again with leather-soled boots or shoes with a low heel are great when you are beginning line dance.

Stepping up

Male and female
If you start studying for medal tests, or belong to a class that does performances, you may want to invest in clothing with more of a cowgirl or cowboy feel and a pair of boots that look good and support your ankles. Otherwise, just keep wearing whatever makes you feel comfortable.

Essential information

1 Line dance has a relaxed, natural stance with knees flexed.

2 The steps are small, neat and relaxed.

3 Women dance with their hands behind their back, or pinching their skirt and men tuck their thumbs tightly into their belt buckles.

4 Loose, relaxed ankles are important. Sit on a chair and try writing the alphabet, one letter at a time in the air with each foot in turn (make sure that you move from your ankle – your knee and thigh should not move). Sit on a hard chair with your back straight – don't slouch!

Health benefits

The line dance movements focus on the feet, ankles, legs and torso, making the dance good for strength and mobility of the lower limbs. The choreographed dances, with changes of direction, help keep the memory working and promote good balance. Doing the same movement at the same time as other people in a group helps create a sense of companionship and well-being.

Fitness level:
Low

Complexity level:
Low

WARNING
Be particularly careful with your knees. If you haven't done much exercise for a while, you may feel some soreness in your thighs and ankles.

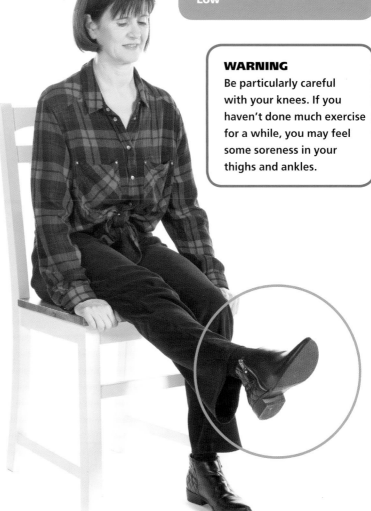

Toe and heel struts

1 Right and left toe struts

- Stand with hands behind back, or tucked into belt.
- Place right foot forward on ball.
- Lower heel so whole foot is on floor, weight on right foot (right toe strut).
- Place left foot forward on ball of foot.
- Lower heel, so whole foot is on floor, weight on left foot (left toe strut).
- Repeat four times (right, left, right, left).

Repeat four times				
PATTERN	Right	Left	Right	Left
TIMING	**1** 2	3 4	5 6	7 8

start position

right toe
1

lower heel
2

2 Add the same pattern placing heel on floor first (heel strut)

- Place heel of right foot forward.
- Lower toe, so whole foot is on floor, weight on right foot (right heel strut).
- Place heel of left foot forward.
- Lower toe, so whole foot is on floor, weight on left foot (left heel strut)
- Repeat four times (right, left, right, left).

Repeat four times				
PATTERN	Right	Left	Right	Left
TIMING	**2** 2	3 4	5 6	7 8

start position

right heel
2

lower foot
2

left toe

3

lower heel

4

HELPFUL HINT
Notice how similar this move is to the toe and heel stamps in tap dance.

left heel

3

lower foot

4

Grapevine right with touch and clap

1 Grapevine to right

- Stand with hands behind back, or in belt.
- Step side right foot, transfer weight.
- Cross left foot, on ball of foot, behind right foot.
- Step side right foot, transfer weight (grapevine).
- Close left foot to right foot, touch ball of left foot to floor (touch) clap hands as you touch.

TECHNIQUE TIP
Keep your head up – it's tempting to look at the floor.

start position

step side right foot

1

2 Add a Grapevine to the left, with a hitch and ¼ turn left

- Step side left foot, transfer weight.
- Cross right foot, on ball of foot, behind left foot.
- Step side left foot, transfer weight (grapevine).
- Lift right knee as you make a ¼ turn left, anti-clockwise to face left side of the room (hitch).
- Repeat whole task four times (so that you dance facing each side of the room).

TECHNIQUE TIP
The way that you are facing at the start of a sequence becomes your front of room for that sequence.

step side left foot

5

cross behind right foot

6

cross behind left foot

2

step side right foot

3

touch left foot and clap

4

step side left foot

7

hitch right foot and ¼ turn left

8

Something harder
◆ Repeat the whole pattern
starting with left foot, making
a ¼ turn right, clockwise,
on the hitch to face the right
side of the room.

Electric Slide by Ric Silvern

Watch the video
Haynes.com/dancemanual

1 Grapevine right and left with scuff

◆ Stand with hands behind back or tucked in belt.
◆ Grapevine right.
◆ Strike left heel into the floor as you close your left leg (scuff).
◆ Repeat grapevine and scuff to left.

Suggested music

◆ *Dance The Night Away,* The Mavericks
◆ *Boot Scootin' Boogie,* Brooks & Dunn

start position

grapevine to right
1 2 3

2 Add three walks back and a touch

◆ Step back right foot.
◆ Step back left foot.
◆ Step back right foot.
◆ Touch left foot to right foot, lean backward from waist.

step back right foot
9

step back left foot
10

scuff
4

repeat to the left side
5 6 7 8

step back right foot
11

touch left foot
12

Electric Slide by Ric Silvern *continued*

3 Add forward touch, back touch

- ◆ Step forward left foot.
- ◆ Touch right foot, lean forward from waist.
- ◆ Step back right foot.
- ◆ Touch left foot, lean backward from waist.

step forward left foot

13

touch right foot

14

step backward right foot

15

touch left foot

16

Something harder
Improvise

- ◆ Relax more into the feel of the music and improvise a few moves to add to the dance.
- ◆ Introduce a turn instead of the grapevine left.
- ◆ Add claps on the touches.

step side left foot

5

step side right foot (½ turn left)

6

4 Add a step left, scuff and hitch with ¼ turn

◆ Step forward left foot.
◆ Scuff right foot forward and make a ¼ turn left with hitch.

Step forward left foot

17

scuff right foot

¼ turn to left with hitch

18

5 Re-start the sequence facing the new wall

◆ Keep repeating until the music finishes, facing a new wall each time you start the sequence

step side left foot (½ turn left)

7

touch or scuff right foot

8

Jazz dance

Jazz dance comes in many guises and has developed as both a social dance style and a theatre form. It has roots in Afro-American culture, tap and the rhythms of jazz music from the late 1800s to mid 1900s.

It has probably developed into more distinct styles than any other dance form and is usually categorised into two broad areas:

1   Traditional jazz, including the Lindy Hop and the Charleston.
2   Theatre jazz, including styles used in Broadway or West End shows, pop concerts and DVDs.

At the end of the 19th century, the Afro-American drum rhythms and the European march met in the sound of ragtime music, and dances that had developed on the plantations, such as the cake walk, had found their way onto the dance floor. Ragtime steps and dances such as the Turkey Trot, Monkey Glide and Bunny Hug continued to liberate the way people danced and it was only a short step from ragtime to the looser structure of jazz music.

The 'break' or 'riff' in jazz music was not only a chance for the musician to improvise and show off their skills but also for the dancers to invent new steps. Dances such as the Black Bottom, the Charleston and the Lindy Hop took ballrooms by storm. Traditional jazz dancers also performed professionally at the Savoy Ballroom and the Cotton Club. Some dancers, such as George 'Shorty' Snowden, became so associated with particular steps that those steps are still named after them today. The Lindy Hop was particularly popular and worked well with the evolving rhythms of swing music. It is often quoted as leading to the jitterbugging dance craze of the 1940s. The term traditional jazz is applied to all of these dances.

Theatre jazz is often broken down into three smaller areas:

1   Broadway jazz, which takes inspiration from musical shows.
2   Commercial jazz, which blends street with more fluid movements.
3   Modern jazz, which blends the isolations and syncopation of jazz with contemporary dance styles

It was an easy transition for jazz dancers from Vaudiville shows to Broadway Musicals and Hollywood films. Choreographers also thrived, with Jerome Robbins,

Matt Mattox and Bob Fosse leaving their own stamps on jazz dance and its development. Jerome Robbins combined ballet with jazz steps and his choreography in *West Side Story* (1957) is still considered a masterpiece. Matt Mattox trained with Jack Cole, who is often considered to be the Father of Jazz. Mattox took many of the moves that he learned and used them as a basis for his own technique, which is now taught around the world. Bob Fosse created a style focusing on hip isolations and rounded shoulders with isolated arm and hand movements. Films such as *Sweet Charity* (1969), *Cabaret* (1972), *All That Jazz* (1979) and *Chicago* (2002) based on popular musicals ensure that his technique is seen and loved by many people.

Commercial jazz is used in pop and commercial videos. Stars such as Beyoncé, Jennifer Lopez, Janet Jackson and of course Michael Jackson have been key players in reinventing the form that now combines various street dance styles with more fluid movements. By contrast, modern jazz dance blends the isolations and rhythms from

Jazz dance and music

Jazz dance plays with the syncopation of the music, working with the 'off' beats as well as the 'main' beats. As with tap dancing, the rhythm is more dominant in the movement than the melody.

Jazz music has a distinctive rhythm and phrasing that evolved from ragtime. There are, however, many different genres of jazz music, including Bebop, Blues, Dixieland, Swing and West Coast (plus many more). Jazz music now appears in many styles which influences mainstream music.

jazz with more contemporary theatre dance styles. The practice tasks and sequence in this section are based on Broadway jazz dance styles.

As with all dance styles in the 21st century, jazz continues to evolve at a pace, not only blending its own different strands but being strongly influenced by changes in other emerging styles around it.

The Jazz dance class

Adult jazz classes are sometimes advertised to focus on a particular type of jazz, but often the teacher will blend elements of all three types of theatre jazz dance in a way and at a pace that is appropriate for class members. Attend a local class with an open mind and give it a go, or chat with the teacher and look at their website before you attend. Classes usually last about an hour and often take inspiration from West End shows and dance films, teaching routines to hits from the shows. Jazz classes are usually full of energy and exciting uplifting music.

A jazz dance class will always start with a good warm-up to strengthen the body and improve flexibility then it will also work on moving different parts of the body in isolation. The class will include short sequences of movement and usually finish with a class dance built up over a number of weeks. This is so class members can start to remember the steps and relax and enjoy dancing a bit more. The teacher will always lead a cool-down before the class ends.

Dress code

Adult jazz classes often have a fairly relaxed dress code, as long as class members are safe and can move easily. Some classes are taught in bare feet, but generally dancers wear jazz shoes, which are tight-fitting leather lace-up shoes with very small heels and flexible soles or special dance trainers, which are lighter and more flexible than ordinary

training shoes. Never wear trainers or any thick rubber-soled shoes, sandals, or shoes with platforms or wedge heels, as this will be very frustrating and make dancing difficult and unsafe for you.

As you improve, you will want to buy specialist shoes – these must fit well. There is an increasing range of designs available, so ask for advice when you are ready to buy a pair and/or try on a range of styles before you finally decide what to buy. Class teachers will often help you find a pair of shoes that suit your feet as well as your budget. Good manufacturers include Bloch, Sansha and Capezio.

Starting out

Female
Basic fitness clothes or leggings and a T-shirt are a good way to start. It's a good idea to tie your hair back if it's long so that it's out of the way. You will need either a pair of jazz shoes or bare feet.

Male
Wear loose-fitting trousers, such as tracksuit bottoms, or shorts with a T-shirt or fitted shirt. You will need either a pair of jazz shoes or bare feet.

Stepping up

Male and female
Dancewear doesn't change, but as you progress you may want to invest in a pair of jazz shoes. You may also want to buy specific 'jazz pants' that are designed to give a good line to the leg.

Essential information

1 In jazz, the centre of gravity is up, although there is a sense of moving into the floor from below the waist, and the knees are flexed.

2 You should feel like your upper body wants to move upwards, your bottom half wants to move towards the floor. Your stomach should be your centre and it should guide the rest of your body.

3 Jazz dance requires the dancer to move different parts of the body in isolation. This takes a lot of practise.

4 Tasks are performed starting with the right foot and then repeated starting with the left foot to ensure that the body is worked evenly.

1st (parallel) position

5 Jazz dance echoes the syncopated rhythms in traditional jazz music.

6 Three basic positions used are: 1st (also known as parallel), 2nd and 4th.

2nd position

4th position

Practice task 1
Bounces and flick kicks

1 Start with bounces

- Stand in parallel, feel like your upper body wants to move upwards, your bottom half wants to move towards the floor, knees flexed.
- Gently bend both legs at the same time to create a little bounce (only move about 1cm).
- Repeat eight times.

> **WARNING**
> Be gentle with your knees. Do not do strong bounces; they should be very gentle, small movements.

start position

bounce

return to start position

1

2 Add a step across and point

- Step across body with right foot in front of left foot, both knees bent.
- Point left foot to side, straighten right leg.
- Step across body with left foot in front of right foot, both knees bent.
- Close right foot to left foot (back to parallel).
- Repeat whole task four times, starting each set of 'step across and point' with alternate feet.

> **TECHNIQUE TIP**
> Try and keep your hips as level as possible as you do this step.

start position

step across right foot

2 2

Remember

◆ Do the general warm-ups before tackling this section.
◆ Practise each section of the practice tasks separately before joining it onto another section.
◆ Repeat the whole task several times when you have joined all of the sections together.
◆ Refresh your memory of the abbreviations by looking at the introduction again.

Repeat eight times								
PATTERN	Bounce	Bounce	Bounce	Bounce	Bounce	Bounce	Bounce	Bounce
TIMING	**1**	2	3	4	5	6	7	8

HELPFUL HINT
Take 1 count for each gentle bounce.

point left foot
3 4

step across left foot
5 6

return to parallel
7 8

Rib isolations

1 Rib isolations to the side

- ◆ Stand in parallel with knees bent hands on hips. Move ribcage to right side, keeping rest of body still.
- ◆ Return ribcage to original position (centre).
- ◆ Move ribcage to left side, keeping rest of body still.
- ◆ Return ribcage to original position (centre).

start position

ribcage right

2 Add rib isolations forward and backward

- ◆ Push ribcage forward.
- ◆ Return ribcage centre.
- ◆ Push ribcage backward.
- ◆ Return ribcage centre.

TECHNIQUE TIP
The movement to the back will naturally be smaller than the other movements.

start position

ribcage forward

Something harder
Variation

Move ribs in each of the directions (right side, forward, left side, backward) and then make the move continuous so that it feels and looks as if your ribs are moving in a circle – of course, everything else is perfectly still!

Don't forget to start the task moving your ribcage to the left as well as the right. Repeat the task eight times in each direction to build strength and flexibility.

HELPFUL HINT
It is really helpful to do this task in front of a mirror so you can see when your ribs move.

start position

ribcage right

HELPFUL HINT
Imagine a piece of
string pulling your ribs
from one side to another,
try to keep everything
else very still.

ribcage centre

ribcage left

ribcage centre

ribcage centre

ribcage backward

ribcage centre

TECHNIQUE TIP
The movement may
be quite small at
first, but it will get
bigger the more you
practise it.

ribcage forward

ribcage left

ribcage backward

Broadway jazz sequence

Watch the video
Haynes.com/dancemanual

1 Flick and step behind-side-in front

◆ Stand in parallel, facing front of the room.
◆ Flick right foot to side, bend left Leg, extend arms to the side and flick both wrists.
◆ Step on ball of right foot behind left foot.
◆ Step side on ball of left foot.
◆ Cross right foot in front of left foot, transfer full weight onto flat right foot, left foot on ball with minimal weight.

◆ Repeat starting with left foot (flick with left foot from this position).
◆ Flick left foot to side, bend right leg, extend arms to the side and flick both wrists.
◆ Step on ball of left foot behind right foot.
◆ Step side on ball of right foot.
◆ Step left foot in front of right foot, transfer full weight onto the flat left foot, right foot on ball with minimal weight.

start position

right foot flick
1

step right foot behing left foot (ball)
2

2 Add four spring ball changes with arms in opposition

◆ Spring so right foot moves to where left foot is (cut).
◆ Left foot to side on ball of foot, briefly transfer weight onto the ball of left foot.
◆ Return full weigh to right foot (ball change).
◆ Let arms swing naturally as if walking (opposition).
◆ Repeat four times alternating feet (right, left, right, left).

Spring ball change			
PATTERN	Spring onto flat right foot	Transfer weight onto left foot	Return weight to flat right foot
TIMING	2	&	2

spring ball change right foot
2 & 2

spring ball change left foot
3 & 4

Suggested music

◆ *New York, New York*, Frank Sinatra
◆ *The Pink Panther Theme*, Henry Mancini and his Orchestra

step left foot

3

step right foot in front (flat)

4

repeat starting left foot

5 6 7 8 to left

spring ball change right foot

5 & 6

spring ball change left foot

7 & 8

Broadway jazz sequence *continued*

3 Add step back, together, step kick

◆ Step back right foot, transferring weight onto it.

◆ Bring left foot back to join right foot in parallel.

◆ Step forward right foot.

◆ Kick left foot.

◆ Repeat starting with left foot (step back left foot immediately from the kick).

> **WARNING**
> Start with the kick quite low then take it higher as you get stronger and more flexible.

step back right foot

3

step back left foot so feet are together

2

4 Add step forward and backward

◆ Step forward right foot to face right corner, front of room knee bent, right arm to side, broken at elbow.

◆ Step left foot, bringing it parallel to right foot, left arm to side broken at elbow.

◆ Step back right foot, transfer weight, bend left knee, place right hand on hip.

◆ Step back on left foot bringing it parallel to right foot, place left hand on hip.

step forward right foot

4

step left foot bringing feet together

2

TECHNIQUE TIP
As you get stronger, go on to the balls of your feet as you step backwards.

step forward right foot

3

kick left leg

4

repeat starting with left foot

5 6 7 8

TECHNIQUE TIP
Keep your arms strong and try to move from the elbow, keeping your shoulders still.

step back right foot

3

step back left foot to bring feet together

4

Broadway jazz sequence *continued*

5 **Add Jazz hands and step ready to repeat the sequence starting left foot**

- Lift arms to side, with jazz hands, turn from waist so that upper body faces front.
- Step left foot to face front, step right foot to return to parallel position, facing front of the room, lower hands.
- Repeat sequence starting with left foot.

jazz hands

5 6

step left foot, then right foot into parallel

7 8

Something harder
Add a prop

- Add a prop, such as a cane, when you dance the routine.
- Change the last eight counts, take the cane in the right hand, place it on the floor and walk around it.

HELPFUL HINT
Have the knob of the cane facing the direction of the foot that you are going to use to start the sequence.

cane on floor

4

walk round the cane to face front

2

Extra practise

Practise bending your knees at the same time as turning in your waist, so that your body above the waist faces the front of the room (or as much as possible) whilst your hips, knees and feet keep facing the front corner of the room. Remember to practise on both sides.

feet together, legs straight

bend knees and twist from the waist so upper body faces front of the room

bring feet together, hold cane

3   4   5   6   7   8

Flamenco dance

Flamenco dance continues to capture the imagination of holidaymakers in Spain and people who fall in love with the language and culture. It is often thought of as the folk dance of Spain, but it is generally accepted that flamenco developed in the 15th century forges of southern Spain.

Gypsies worked as blacksmiths and the original flamenco songs developed accompanied only by rhythms made within the forges. The haunting sounds of these songs are a blend of Arabic, Iraqi, Iranian, Greek, Turkish and Indian influences. The song (el Cante) is still regarded as the most important part of flamenco. The guitar (Toque) and dance (el Baile) were only added in the 18th century.

For centuries, flamenco remained the music for gypsies and poor people and a local attraction for those undertaking the Grand Tour of Europe. The Concorra National (a competition held in 1922) propelled flamenco into the national and international arena, and it quickly spread, not only in popularity but also becoming accepted as an art form. The rapid growth of the package-holiday industry in the 1970s further raised its profile with the many tourists visiting Spain. This growth of interest sparked a period of intense experimentation and evolution for flamenco music, with guitarists such as Paco de Lucía and Paco Peña having chart entries in the UK and the singer Camarón de La Isla gaining rock-star status.

Although flamenco can be seen across Spain today, its heartland remains in Jerez, Cadiz, Triana and Seville. Flamenco is about doing and expressing how you feel in the moment, not about performing beautiful positions for a passive audience. Flamenco is a solo dance and includes hand clapping and percussive footwork, contrasted with lyrical, intricate hand, arm and body movements.

The men's and women's dances are very similar. The footwork is the same, but men use their arms more forcefully and hold their fingers straight rather than doing the more flowery twisting movements used by the women. Often the hands are moving continuously during the dance in contrast to the percussive footwork.

The percussive footwork, central to flamenco, comprises three ways of tapping:

1 The whole foot hits the floor (planta)
2 Only the toes hit the floor (punta)
3 Only the heel hits the floor (tacon).

Usually flamenco dancers don't find their voice until they reach thirty years old and it is not unusual for professional dancers to still be performing in their fifties. At social events older women are often encouraged to dance as unlike in most styles, older dancers are highly respected. Maturity and life experience as well as mastery of flamenco rthymns brings a depth to their performance communicating the highly prized expression of *el duende* (the soul of inner self). It is often said that young dancers cannot communicate this as they have not had enough life experience.

Flamenco is enjoying a resurgence of interest across the UK and America. In London, Sadler's Wells holds an annual flamenco festival, which showcases the latest trend of mixing dance styles to make a new vocabulary. Leading exponents today include Farruquito, Eva Yerbabuena and Joaquín Cortés. Each is experimenting and developing Flamenco in their own way. Farruquito keeps the improvised nature of the past but blends this with a modern vocabulary, Yerabuena combines flamenco dance with western contemporary theatre forms and Cortés combines flamenco, ballet and contemporary dance in ever changing ways.

Flamenco dance and music

It is sometimes easier to think of flamenco dance being part of the music rather than something that happens with the music. The feet become percussion instruments and the clapping is often referred to as the metronome for the performers, not dominating but keeping a beat to help the other performers.

There are two types of claps:

1 Hard (fuertes) made by hitting the palm of one hand with three fingers from the other hand, making a crisp and sharp sound.
2 Soft (sordas) made by cupping both hands and clapping.

The clapper accents different beats within the music to indicate which rhythm to use to the dancer and musicians. The accents in the music are central to flamenco, so much so that it can be said that without accents there is no flamenco.

Flamenco music is classified by song style (or cante) and has a strong framework within which the singer, musicians and dancer work together so each has a time to shine. If you like flamenco and want to really explore the dance style, you will need to become very familiar with the different musical structures and how they work with the dance. The basic flamenco rhythms are: Tango flamenco, solea, alegia, seguriguia, bulerias and rumbas.

The Flamenco class

Flamenco classes may be a group dance class or a partnered dance class. Classes usually last for an hour. The energy created by the stamping and clapping often makes them exciting and very social.

Classes will always start with a warm-up and will then work on basic posture, arm and foot positions and co-ordination of hand and foot movements. The teacher will introduce simple sequences of basic movements working to the various rhythms in flamenco. The class will usually finish with a class dance built up over a number of weeks so class members start to remember the steps and patterns and to bring their own style to the moves. The teacher will always lead a cool-down before the class ends.

As you get more experienced and gain greater understanding of the rhythms you will be able to do the footwork more quickly, developing light and shade in the footwork and your own style and flair.

The Spanish Dance Society is the biggest dance organisation supporting flamenco teachers and has offices in many countries; as such, many teachers follow the syllabus that it has developed. Although some classes may cater for

all levels, classes are usually offered at beginner, improver and intermediate levels.

Le Sevillanas, a popular dance with a light feel and quite basic rhythms can be seen widely throughout Spain and is often taught at beginner classes. Some teachers offer day or weekend courses that provide the opportunity to immerse yourself in the dance style.

Dress code

Adult flamenco dance classes usually have a fairly strict dress code. The skirt is important for female dancers, as it is often used within movements so it needs to be full enough for you to be able to lift it up to the sides. The key, however, is to have appropriate footwear. Neither men nor women need to invest in flamenco shoes for the first lesson, but it is important to wear a hard-soled shoe with a heel that fits securely, otherwise you will not be able to make the percussive feet sounds. Never wear trainers or any rubber-soled shoes, sandals, or shoes with platforms or wedge heels, as this will be very frustrating and make dancing difficult and unsafe for you.

As you improve, you will want to buy flamenco shoes. It is best to chat with a teacher as they usually have a relationship with a particular manufacturer (or two) and will help you buy the correct shoes when the time is right. Gallardo and Senovilla are good makes and Osuna is great for a basic shoe. Flamenco dresses are not usually worn in class but are fun if the class does a performance.

Starting out

Female
A lightweight calf-length flared skirt or trousers are ideal. However, a fitted top with leggings and a large fringed shawl tied around the waist is all that you need to get started. A well-fitting shoe with a strap or T-bar and a low-to-medium chunky heel, or a simple court shoe is great for the beginner.

Male
Wear a lightweight shirt and trousers – jeans are not a good idea, as they do not stretch. A hard-soled shoe with a small heel will get you started.

Stepping up

Female
Investing in a well-made pair of flamenco shoes is probably the most important thing for someone who wants to really get to grips with flamenco. Practice dresses and skirts give a a feel for the movement, and accessories like flowers and combs for the hair, fans and castanets add to the feel for the dance.

Male
Invest in a well-made pair of flamenco boots (with a heel and metallic nails at the toes) so that you can practise properly. You may also want to buy a pair of lightweight trousers, short enough to show off the footwork.

Essential information

1 Basic posture is important. Push down from your hips and pull up from the waist, flex your knees slightly and ensure your weight is over both feet equally. Hold your head high and proud. Both hands form a fist at the waist.

2 Flamenco dance needs strong and angular arms. Keep tension in your arms and hands.

3 Flamenco uses contra positions, (e.g. your head looks right and your body faces left).

Health benefits

The stamping and strong legwork makes flamenco particularly good for maintaining bone density in the lower body and for strengthening the calves, hamstrings and thighs. When moving at quick speeds, flamenco is a good cardiovascular exercise.

Fitness level:
Moderate

Complexity level:
High

WARNING
Be particularly careful with your calves, thighs, neck and shoulders.

4 Practise clapping to help you gain a deeper understanding of flamenco rhythm. Listen and clap to Solo Compas, such as the ones suggested on page 101.

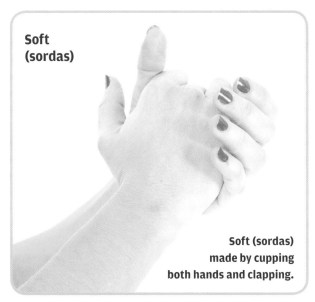

Soft (sordas)

Soft (sordas) made by cupping both hands and clapping.

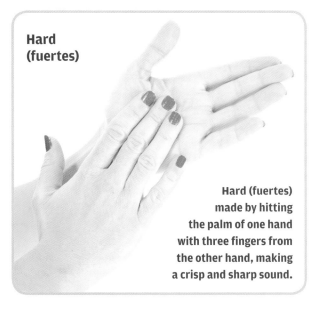

Hard (fuertes)

Hard (fuertes) made by hitting the palm of one hand with three fingers from the other hand, making a crisp and sharp sound.

Claps and stamps

Clap a tango flamenco rhythm

♦ To help you get the right feel stand in your posture with your hands on your waist, fingers together (men would stand with palms on your lungs, just below your chest).

♦ Clap the rhythm below.

TECHNIQUE TIP
The quality and consistency of the tone of your claps is far more important than the speed.

HELPFUL HINT
Keep tension in your arms and wrists as you clap. Repeat the rhythm until you are confident.

Repeat								
PATTERN	X	Clap	Clap	Clap	X	Clap-clap	Clap	Clap
TIMING	1	2	3	4	5	6	7	8

Practice task 2

1 Stamps (glope) and claps (in eight steady counts)

♦ Stand in a good flamenco posture. Feet together, hold skirt with one hand then place it on waist so that skirt is lifted a little.

♦ Lift right leg from knee, behind you. Remember the leg you are standing on should be slightly bent.

♦ Bring right foot down to original place, putting whole foot flat on floor, producing a sharp and crisp sound (glope).

♦ Transfer weight onto right foot, so that left foot is ready to move.

Repeat eight times								
PATTERN	Right	Left	Right	Left	Right	Left	Right	Left
TIMING	& 1	& 2	& 3	& 4	& 5	& 6	& 7	& 8

WARNING
Make sure that you start each glope with your thigh facing downward towards the floor and your foot behind you; DO NOT lift your foot with your knee up and in the front, as this is harmful to your knees and you will not make the right sound.

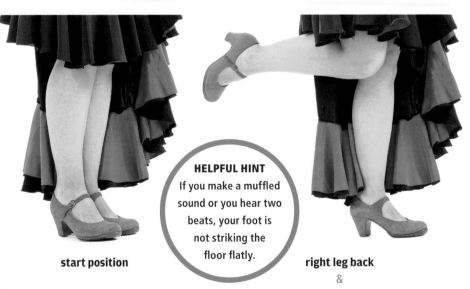

HELPFUL HINT
If you make a muffled sound or you hear two beats, your foot is not striking the floor flatly.

start position

right leg back

&

Glopes to the tango flamenco rhythm

- Perform glopes to the tango flamenco rhythm.
- Remember to clap the tango rhythm at the start to indicate your rhythm and speed.

TECHNIQUE TIP
Make sure that you transfer your weight fully onto the foot that has stamped on the floor so that the other leg is free for the next movement; otherwise you will not be able to dance at speed.

REMEMBER
Your double stamp can only take one beat in total, so your movements will need to be small.

Repeat								
PATTERN	X	Right foot stamp	Left foot stamp	Right foot stamp	X	Left foot – Right foot stamp	Left foot stamp	Right foot stamp
TIMING	1	2	3	4	5	6	7	8

2 Add four sordas (soft) claps

- Add four sordas (soft) claps at the start to indicate the speed at which you are going to dance.

TECHNIQUE TIP
Your head should not bounce up and down as you make the steps – check that you are moving on one level.

Remember

- Do the general warm-ups before tackling this section.
- Practise each section of the practice tasks separately before joining it onto another section.
- Repeat the whole task several times when you have joined all of the sections together.
- Refresh your memory of the abbreviations by looking at the Introduction again.
- If you are not familiar with flamenco music, use a metronome, simple steady drum beat or no music for the first two tasks, so you don't have to worry about getting the rhythm from the music.

stamp

1

Suggested music

- *Como El Agua*, Camarón De La Isla
- *Tangos de Pepico*, Estrella Morente
- *Tangos de le Plaza*, Enrique Morente

Strengthening arms and wrists

1 Wrist and hand basic movement – 'Picking Apples from a Tree'

◆ Stand in a good flamenco stance.
◆ Stretch right arm in front, palm upwards, hold elbow with left hand.
◆ Circle wrist inwards, imagine you are picking an apple and let your middle finger bend slightly further than your other fingers.
◆ Keeping hold of apple, leading with the middle finger, continue to circle wrist so that hand faces down to the floor.
◆ Continue circle so that wrist turns outwards, still holding apple.
◆ When hand as gone as far as it can, let apple go with a flick to straighten fingers.
◆ Repeat four times with right hand and then four times with left hand.

hold right elbow

circle wrist in

2 Add four arm reaches up and down

◆ Stand in a good flamenco stance, right hand at waist but not in a fist.
◆ Raise right arm above head, circling wrist, keeping elbow above hand for as long as possible.
◆ When arm is as high as you can get it bend wrist, still holding your apple.
◆ Reverse process to lower arm. Remember to keep elbow high.
◆ Repeat four times using right arm and then four times with left arm (right, right, right, right, left, left, left, left).

TECHNIQUE TIP
Move in your own time, making the movements fluid and elegant and make full circles with your wrists.

start position

arm up elbow lead

wrist down

wrist up

flick at end

keep elbow high for as long as possible

reverse pattern down

return to start

Flamenco

Watch the video
Haynes.com/dancemanual

1 Clap the tango flamenco rhythm

◆ Stand in basic posture with hands on waist to start.

◆ Clap rhythm twice to set tempo for sequence (first clap on count 2).

REMEMBER
Counts one and five are always silent.

start position

clap

PATTERN	X	Clap	Clap	Clap	X	Clap-clap	Clap	Clap
TIMING	1	2	3	4	5	6	7	8
REPEAT	2	2	3	4	5	6	7	8

2 Add right knee lift

◆ Lift right knee up, gripping skirt with right hand as it lifts.

◆ Bring hands together, still holding skirt, put them next to each other on right side of waist, maintain posture.

◆ Twist shoulders, bringing left shoulder forward and look over that shoulder turning head, giving a contra position.

right knee lift (skirt lifted)
3 2 3 4

place hands together on right of waistband
5 6 7 8

3 Add stamps

- Stamp the tango flamenco rhythm twice. Start with right foot then repeat, starting with the left foot.

4 Repeat whole sequence

- Remember the speed that you clap is the speed that you will dance the sequence.

Suggested music

- *Como El Agua*, Camarón De La Isla
- *Tangos de Pepico*, Estrella Morente
- *Tangos de le Plaza*, Enrique Morente

PATTERN	X	Right foot stamp	Left foot stamp	Right foot stamp	X	Left foot stamp – Right foot stamp	Left foot stamp	Right foot stamp
TIMING	4	2	3	4	5	6	7	8
PATTERN	X	Left foot stamp	Righ stamp	Left foot stamp	X	Right foot stamp – Left foot stamp	Right foot stamp	Left foot stamp
TIMING	5	2	3	4	5	6	7	8

Something harder
That flamenco feel

- Stand on right foot to start with left foot a little forward on ball of foot, look over right shoulder, skirt tucked into left side of waistband.
- Clap tango flamenco rhythm to set the tempo.
- Lift left knee and take hands to right side of skirt.
- Stamp the rhythm twice. Start with right foot then repeat starting with left foot.
- To finish, stamp and clap the tango flamenco rhythm at the same time. Start with right foot and then repeat starting with left foot.

PATTERN FEET	X	Right foot stamp	Left foot stamp	Right foot stamp	X	Left foot stamp – Right foot stamp	Left foot stamp	Right foot stamp
PATTERN HANDS	X	Clap	Clap	Clap	X	Clap-clap	Clap	Clap
TIMING	6	2	3	4	5	6	7	8
PATTERN FEET	X	Left foot stamp	Right foot stamp	Left foot stamp	X	Righ foot stamp – Left foot stamp	Right foot stamp	Left foot stamp
PATTERN HANDS	X	Clap	Clap	Clap	X	Clap-clap	Clap	Clap
TIMING	7	2	3	4	5	6	7	8

Ballet

Ballet is one of the most popular dance forms, with the ballet class still being a key part of growing up for many girls. Ballet performances continue to attract big audiences and companies tour worldwide.

Ballet developed in the Renaissance Courts of Italy in the 15th and 16th centuries, spreading across Europe to France where dances were performed at court by royalty, nobility and foreign dignitaries (all men of course!). These big spectacles – known as 'Court Ballets' – included singing, poetry and drama, as well as dance. They were embraced in the French Court of King Louis XIV, whose love of dance was well known. Throughout his reign, ballet flourished; women started to perform, he founded the first school of Ballet at the Paris Opera and began to codify the steps and positions. His influence is clear and ballet steps are still known by French names throughout the world today.

In the late 19th century, the centre of ballet moved from France to Russia. The partnership between the composer Pyotr Ilyich Tchaikovsky and Marius Petitpa, the ballet master at the Imperial Russian Theatre in St Petersburg, led to the creation of some of the most famous ballets including *Swan Lake*, *Sleeping Beauty* and *The Nutcracker*, which remain three of the most popular ballets today.

Russia's dominance continued into the 20th century, thanks largely to the dance impresario (organiser) Sergei Diaghilev, who was manager of the Ballet Russe Theatre. Many of the dancers in the Ballet Russe Company had been members of the Tsar's Imperial Ballet of St Petersburg. Their training gave them a powerful and physical style of dancing which, together with modern choreography by Vaslav Nijinsky, took ballet into a new era. When the company toured Europe and London in 1911 people did not know whether to be shocked or amazed! Such was the influence of Ballet Russe that many of the dancers went on to found a number of the leading ballet companies that are still performing today. Ninette De Valois founded Sadler's Wells Ballet (now the Royal Ballet), Marie Rambert founded Ballet Rambert (now Rambert Dance Company), Mikhail Mordkin founded The Morkin Ballet (now American Ballet Theatre) and George Balanchine became director of New York City Ballet.

The pointe shoe is one of the defining features of the female ballet dancer. Pointe shoes are soft, close-fitting slippers with a hardened toe. They make many steps

Ballet and music

Typically, ballet has a very literal and narrative relationship with the musical score where the steps work closely with the melody and rhythm, following the phrasing of the music. Although not always the case, ballet companies still often commission music and the choreographer and composer collaborate closely as the ballet is created.

The *Dance of the Cygnets* in *Swan Lake* and the *Clog Dance* in *La Fille Mal Gardée* have both gained popularity beyond their part in the ballets because of the special relationship between the music and choreography.

possible that, for technical reasons, could not be done on demi-pointe (tip-toe). There are many myths surrounding their development, although they are believed to have first appeared in a performance at the Paris Opera as long ago as 1818. The pointe shoe gives all female ballet dancers the appearance of floating in the air and, although painful to wear, they quickly became a permanent feature of ballet. Each shoe has a maker's mark and once a dancer finds pointe shoes that fit well, they will buy shoes by the same maker. Pointe shoes make the training and strength needed to be a ballet dancer challenging and many young girls are still injured by dancing on pointe before they have the strength and technique necessary to do so.

The roles of male and female ballet dancers are very specific. The male ballet dancer's role has always focused

on athleticism and power with lots of turns and jumps. Many traditional ballets require them to partner the ballerinas in a way that shows the ballerina to their best effect, which often made the male role appear less demanding than it is.

As ballet continues to evolve and find ways to connect with the world in the 21st century, choreographers sometimes play with the traditional male and female roles. Ballet is also changing in other ways, with choreographers such as Christopher Wheeldon integrating technology and special effects into performances (such as *Alice's Adventures in Wonderland*). Contemporary choreographers, such as Wayne McGregor, create work for ballet dancers and use contemporary and other dance styles alongside traditional ballet steps.

The great full-length ballets from the 19th and early 20th century, such as *Swan Lake*, *Giselle* and *The Nutcracker*, remain a firm favourite with theatre audiences. And with broadcasting of performances by many opera houses into cinemas around the world, these classics – as well as new ballets – are being seen by more people than ever. The glimpses backstage and outline of the story by leading ballerinas such as Darcy Bussell make these events a great way to see ballet, not only for those who are committed fans but also for those who have not yet been brave enough to attend a live performance.

The ballet class

Adult ballet classes usually last about an hour and always follow the same format. Classes start with exercises at the barre – a support for the dancers so they can focus on how their body moves during each exercise. Each exercise is performed twice, once with the left hand and once with the right hand on the barre, so each side of the body is exercised in turn.

The rest of the class happens without the barre, and is known as centre work. This includes a number of exercises, developing the strength, balance and co-ordination needed to be a ballet dancer. This usually includes port de bras (arm positions), adage (slow work), pirouettes (turns), batterie (small fast beats of the feet) and grand allegro (big jumps). Throughout the centre work the teacher puts steps together to produce phrases or sentences of dance known as enchaînement. The teacher will lead a cool-down at the end of the class that always ends with a reverence (curtsey or bow).

Dress code

Most ballet classes – even those for adults – have a strict dress code. Ballet relies on creating a particular line so traditionally ballet dancers wear a leotard and tights with their hair pulled back in a bun and no jewellery so that nothing distracts from the shapes that their bodies make. It is important that the dancer can see the shapes that they are making in a mirror and that the teacher can see that the muscles are working correctly and the body properly aligned. This is partly for aesthetic reasons, but is also to keep the dancers safe. For safety reasons it is important that clothes are not too baggy, even when you are a new learner.

Ballet shoes are usually worn, although it is acceptable to dance with bare feet for the first few lessons until you decide that it is the class for you. Ballet shoes are made from soft leather and need to fit closely like a glove. More experienced dancers fix ribbons to their shoes, but it is best to use a piece of elastic when you first start. Some makes come with the elastic already in position but you can easily fix your own by folding in the heel of the shoe and fixing the elastic where the edge of the shoe touches.

Starting out

Female

Leggings and a fitted T-shirt are fine when you start attending ballet classes, as leotard and tights are very unforgiving! Hair should be off the face and tied back. You will need a pair of ballet shoes, although it is acceptable to dance in bare feet for the first lesson or two.

Male

Shorts and a T-shirt are ideal; it is not obligatory to wear tights. Bare feet are acceptable, but preferably either white or black ballet shoes, usually worn with a pair of short socks.

Stepping up

Female

If you want to attend ballet classes regularly, you will need to wear a leotard and tights so that you and the teacher can see how your body is working. Teenagers and adults often wear a short ballet skirt or a soft fabric tunic that makes them feel less vulnerable but still enables the teacher to see how their body is working.

Male

The basic clothing doesn't change, although you may want to invest in a dance belt and ballet shoes.

Essential information

1 Turnout is a key feature of ballet. This is when you turn your legs out from the hip, keeping your knees over your toes. An easy way to check this is to stand in first position and bend your knees, keeping your heels on the floor (demi plié). Your knees must be over your toes. If they are not, keep turning your feet in until they are.

2 In ballet, your weight needs to be over your toes and slightly forward. Stand up straight and pull up out of your waist towards the ceiling. Imagine someone is pulling a string from the top of your head.

3 Trained dancers work in fifth position. Beginners use third position because it requires less strength and turnout. Remember you still need to turnout from your hips with your knees over your toes. Keep checking and if they are not – turn in your toes.

4 Tasks are performed starting with the right foot and then repeated starting with the left foot to ensure that the body is worked evenly.

WARNING
Be particularly careful with your knees and hips. The amount of turnout you have is mainly due to your natural physique, and for safety all dancers need to work within their turnout range.

There are five basic positions of the feet

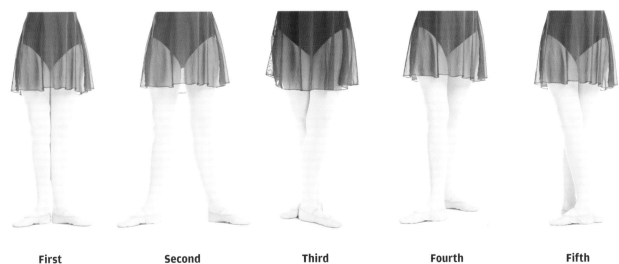

| First | Second | Third | Fourth | Fifth |

Demi pliés with rise

1 Demi plié (small bend of the knees)

◆ Stand in first position, left hand lightly on back of chair, right arm to side (second position).
◆ Push into floor as you bend your knees as far as you can, heels on floor, knees over toes (demi plié).
◆ Press into floor to straighten legs and return to start position.

Suggested music

◆ *Wonderful Tonight*, Eric Clapton
◆ *Patience*, Take That
◆ *Thinking Out Loud*, Ed Sheeran

start position

bend
1 2

stretch
3 4

Something harder

Add a full plié

◆ Replace the first set of demi plié and rise, with a full plié:
◆ Make a demi plié.
◆ Continue pushing into floor, peeling heels off (full plié), lower right arm keeping a slight curved shape (bras bas).
◆ Press into floor, lower heels as soon as possible, back to demi plié, right arm lifts to chest level (first position). Imagine you are holding a large ball.
◆ Press into floor to straighten legs, return to start position, right arm second.
◆ Complete task with 3 x demi pliés and rise.

start position   **demi plié**

PATTERN	Full plié	Demi plié	Rise and lower	Demi plié	Rise and lower	Demi plié	Rise and lower
TIMING	**1** 2 3 4 5 6 7 8	**2** 2 3 4	5 6 7 8	**3** 2 3 4	5 6 7 8	**4** 2 3 4	5 6 7 8

2 Add a rise

◆ Peel feet off floor from heels rising to tip toe (demi-pointe).
◆ Lower heels slowly, imagine that you stay the same height.
◆ Repeat whole task four times.
◆ Turn around and repeat whole task four times holding chair with right hand.

Remember

◆ Do the general warm ups before tackling this section.
◆ Practise each section of the practice tasks separately before joining it onto another section.
◆ Repeat the whole task several times when you have joined all of the sections together.

WARNING
Make sure you use something strong enough to support you as your 'barre'.

rise
5 6

lower
7 8

x4

HELPFUL HINT
To get the head positions, look at your right hand as it moves through the positions.

full plié

demi plié

straighten legs

Tendu front and side

1 Prepare arm

◆ Stand in first position, place left hand lightly on the chair.
◆ Take right arm through first position and out to second, look at arm as it moves, leave head looking towards the corner.
◆ Hold arm in second (Preparation).

HELPFUL HINT
Imagine you have something sticky on the bottom of your shoe and it is making it hard to point your foot.

start position

prepare arm 1st position

prepare arm 2nd position

2 Add four tendu front and four tendu side

◆ Point right foot front, keep contact with floor all of the time, keep turn out.
◆ Close foot to first position, keep contact with floor, keep turn out (tendu front).
◆ Repeat four times. Return head to look straight ahead fourth time.
◆ Point right foot side, keep contact with floor all of time, keep turnout.
◆ Close foot to first position, keep contact with floor, keep turn out (tendu side).
◆ Repeat four times.

TECHNIQUE TIP
Take 1 count for your foot to go out and 1 count for it to close back into the 1st position.

REMEMBER
Only return head to look straight ahead after the fourth tendu front.

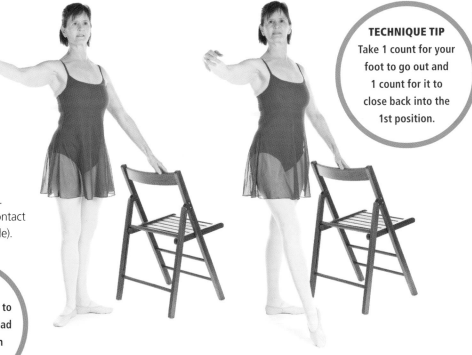

start position   **tendu front**

3 Add two rises to demi-pointe and lower of heels

◆ Rise to demi-pointe.
◆ Lower heels.
◆ Repeat rise and lower.
◆ Repeat whole task twice. After the second time lower right arm to bras bas as you lower your heels.
◆ Turn around and repeat whole task four times holding chair with right hand.

PATTERN	4 tendu front	4 tendu side	rise and lower	rise and lower
TIMING	**1** 2 3 4 5 6 7 8	**2** 2 3 4 5 6 7 8	**3** 2 3 4 5 6 7 8	**4** 2 3 4 5 6 7 8

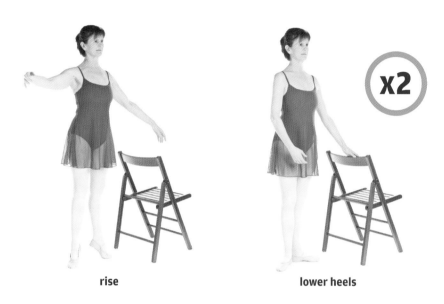

rise   lower heels

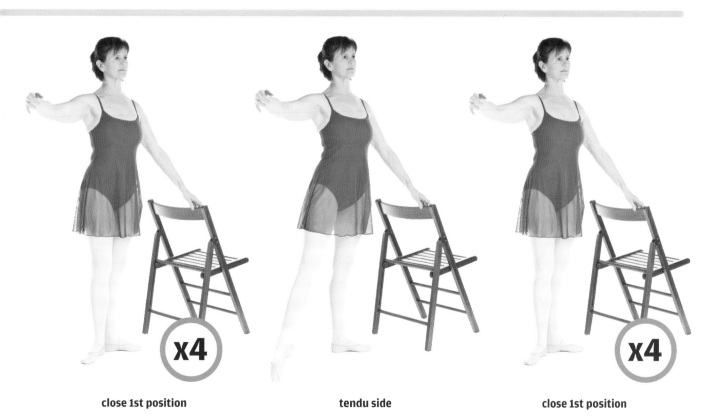

close 1st position   tendu side   close 1st position

Ballet sequence

Watch the video
Haynes.com/dancemanual

1 Balancé forward and backward

- Stand in third position right foot front facing, right corner, front of room, arms in bras bas.
- Step forward right foot putting full weight on foot, right arm in front of body, left arm to side (first arabesque).
- Bring left foot behind right foot, knee bent (flat).
- Briefly transfer weight onto toes of left foot (toe).
- Return full weight to the right foot (balancé forward).
- Step back left foot putting full weight on foot (flat).
- Bring right foot in front of left foot, knee bent, briefly transfer weight onto toes of right foot (toe).
- Return weight to left foot (balancé back).

TECHNIQUE TIP
The transfer of weight is just for an instant. It is the same action as in a ball change in jazz, or bop step in Bollywood.

Start position

Balancé forward step breakdown			
STEP ELEMENT	**Step forward flat right foot**	**Transfer weight to left foot**	**Return to flat right foot**
TIMING	**1**	2	3

2 Add retiré to dégagé right foot

- Lift right foot off floor, making a triangle shape just above ankle (retiré sur le cou-de-pied). Bend left knee.
- Point right foot to side, keeping turn-out (dégagé).
- Take right arm above head, left arm to side (fourth position), eye line down, looking beyond pointed foot.

retiré
&

dégagé
3 2 3

balancé forward
1 2 3

balancé backward
2 2 3

Suggested music
....

◆ *Time To Get Alone,*
  The Beach Boys
◆ *Waltz of the Flowers,*
  Tchaikovsky

HELPFUL HINT
Add these steps together into a smooth sequence and practise starting with your left foot as well as your right foot.

3 Add a pas de bourée (runs)

◆ Place right foot behind left foot as you rise. Weight slightly more on right foot, arms in second.
◆ Step side with left foot, transfer weight slightly left foot, leave arms in second.
◆ Close right foot in front of left foot, demi plié lowering arms to bras bas and looking toward left front room corner.

Pas de bourée
4

2

3

Ballet sequence *continued*

4 Add a dégagé left foot and right foot:

◆ Point left foot to side, straightening right leg, left arm to demi bras (half-way to second).

◆ Close left foot in front of right foot, return arms to bras bas (dégagé left foot).

◆ Point right foot side, right arm to demi bras.

◆ Close right foot in front of left foot, making a demi plié, return arms to bras bas (dégagé right foot).

> **TECHNIQUE TIP**
> When you are confident, look at your hand as you make the arm movement.

dégagé over left foot

5 2

close 3rd position

3

5 Add a relevé and retire

◆ From demi plié snatch feet together as you rise onto demi pointe (relevé).

◆ Lower heels into demi plié.

◆ Relevé lifting left foot to retiré in front of right knee, arms in first position.

◆ Make a 1/8th turn left (anti-clockwise) to face left corner, front of room.

◆ Lower into demi plié, third position, left foot front, arms in first position.

◆ Repeat sequence starting from this position, dancing your balancé on your left foot.

relevé

7 2

demi plié

3

HELPFUL HINT
Think of a string pulling you upwards. This will keep you lifted and make it easier to perform the dégagés.

dégagé over right foot

6 2

close in demi plié, 3rd position

3

retiré (1/8th turn)

8 2

demi plié

3

Something harder
Pirouette

- Replace the last retiré with a pirouette (turn):
- Relevé, left foot retiré and turn right (clockwise) making a 7/8th turn, to face left corner, front of room.
- Lower into demi plié, third position, left foot front, arms in first position.

retiré (7/8th turn)

Bollywood dance

Bollywood dance has become a craze sweeping across Europe, the UK and America, not only raising the profile of the Bollywood film industry but also having a life of its own.

The term Bollywood was first used in the 1970s and is a play on the word Hollywood, with the 'B' coming from Bombay (now known as Mumbai), the centre of film-making in India. Although the dance style has grown in popularity, beyond the connection with Bollywood films it is impossible to separate its development from that of the film industry.

The Bollywood film industry evolved from silent movies based around historical and religious tales; *Raja Harishchandra* (1913) is credited as the first ever Indian feature film. The industry embraced talking films and the 'Golden Age' of Bollywood Films is considered to be the 1940s–1960s. It was during this period that large group dances started to be included in the films, increasing in size, speed and intensity from the 1970s until the now-familiar slick and glamorous style evolved.

Bollywood films contain a mixture of stories, music and dance, which are all components of traditional Indian dance theatre. The structure and appearance of Bollywood films is similar to Hollywood musicals with lavish costumes and sets, and characters suddenly bursting into song and dance. Modern Bollywood films usually include about six song-and-dance numbers. These typically include the hero and/or heroine and a large group of dancers performing fast, exuberant dances in unison (everyone doing the same step at the same time as a whole). Each film has a central song to the story and frequently this is better known than the film itself, often becoming a hit in many countries.

The early Bollywood films used some Indian classical styles such as Bharatanatyam, Kathak and Kathakali, mixed with folk forms such as Bhangra. Each dance style is different but central elements include:

Neck and head movements – a side-to-side neck movement and forward-and-back slide seen across south Asian styles

Facial expressions – known as abhinaya is important. The eyes and eyebrows are used extensively to help portray emotions such as anger, sadness, happiness and love through facial expressions.

Hand movements – known as hastas or mudras, act as a form of sign language to help tell a story and can show things like emotions, animals, plants or places.

Foot movements – flat, flexed feet are traditionally used in South Asian dance styles

These key characteristics still underpin the Bollywood Dance style, but it has become a fusion of many different styles and is now strongly influenced by hip-hop. This means that choreographers can play with the basic techniques to suit them, the dancers and the film narrative. It also means that although there is consensus about some names for steps, people make up new names such as *Patting the Dog*, *Scratch your Head* and *Changing the Light Bulb*! So don't be surprised if you hear movements called by different names.

Since the 2000s, Bollywood films, music and dance have continued to become more mainstream. Stars such as Madonna and Britney Spears have incorporated Bollywood-inspired dances in their live shows and videos, while films such as *Slumdog Millionaire* (2008) have contributed to the ever-growing interest. The drama, high energy and fusion of styles make Bollywood dance fun and easy to learn. Of course, if you want to become really skilled you will need to master the underlying South Asian dance techniques.

Bollywood dance and music

Bollywood dance works strongly with the rhythm of the music. It often uses the spaces between the beats for movements to give extra accent and emphasis to the movement on the beat of the music. The upper and lower parts of the body often move to different rhythms in the music.

The Bollywood class

Bollywood dance classes try to re-create the uplifting feeling and glamour of Bollywood films – enter into the spirit and let yourself go! Classes usually last about an hour, are energetic and also work on the actress (or actor) within.

Because Bollywood is a fusion of many different dance styles, the content of classes varies depending on the personal skills and preferences of the teacher. They will, however, always include a warm-up, followed by tasks and sequences focusing on specific skills used in the classical and folk South Asian dance techniques that underpin Bollywood. These will include wrist, hand, finger, eye, neck and head movements and footwork. Some of these tasks and sequences will be fused with other dance styles and some with story telling.

The class usually finishes with a choreographed class dance built up over a number of weeks so class members start to remember the steps and can relax and enjoy dancing a bit more. The set routines may be taken from, or inspired by, Bollywood films. The class will always finish with a cool down.

Dress code

Bollywood classes are a chance for glamour and fun. They offer an opportunity to wear bright colours and enjoy the costumes and high energy of the dance style. Classes often develop their own style and people usually become more adventurous in what they wear as they become more familiar with the dance style. New class members often wear comfortable clothing in soft fabrics for the first few sessions. If you are concerned, contact the teacher or check out their website before you attend a class.

Starting out

Female
Wear comfortable clothing such as yoga or gym wear. A T-shirt and leggings are fine to get you started. Bare feet or, if you want to wear shoes, soft-soled shoes that allow your feet to flex and stretch are ideal.

Male
Loose-fitting trousers such as tracksuit bottoms, or shorts with room to move. Bare feet or, if you want to wear shoes, soft-soled shoes that allow your feet to flex and stretch are ideal.

Stepping up

Male and female
The teacher will usually advise you, but what you wear will also depend on other class members and the group as a whole. Popular additions to help you get the feel of Bollywood are getting a henna tattoo, wearing a bindi (bright red dot worn in the centre of the forehead) or adding touches of glamour, such as wearing jewellery.

Essential information

1 The controlled, strong and expressive movements of South Asian classical and folk dance styles underpin Bollywood dance.

2 Bollywood is a high-energy dance style, with big, bold movements.

3 Hand gestures are an important detail to bring expression to Bollywood dance.

Health benefits

Bollywood dance is very good for strengthening arms, hands and wrists because of the strong and precise movements. The bouncing and jumping also strengthens the legs and is good for balance because of the many changes of weight. The exuberant nature of the dance style makes it a good cardiovascular exercise.

Fitness level:
High

Complexity level:
High

Articulation of hands

1 Prayer position

- Arms chest height, fingers close together, middle finger tips of each hand touching, elbows out to the side.
- Push hands together rolling through fingers until you reach prayer position.
- Roll back through hands until both are parallel to floor.
- Repeat four times.

fingers together   **halfway**

2 Add finger touches

- Bend arms upward from elbow so fingers face the ceiling, fingers as strong and straight as possible, touch first finger and thumb together.
- Touch middle finger and thumb together.
- Touch ring finger and thumb together.
- Touch little finger and thumb together.
- Starting from little finger reverse the task (ring, middle, first).
- Repeat four times.

thumb/first finger   **thumb/middle finger**

3 Add lotus hand position

- Bring hands parallel to floor, palms facing down, fingers stretched as wide as possible.
- Leading with little finger turn palm over, keep thumb and first finger as straight, wide and flat as possible, allowing the other fingers to curl over.
- Return to parallel, leading with little finger.
- Repeat four times.

hands parallel to floor

HELPFUL HINT
If your hands and fingers start to ache, give them a good shake to relax them and build up gradually to doing the full task.

prayer position

open prayer

thumb/ring finger

thumb/little finger

halfway

lotus

Hip shakes and hand twists

1 Right hip shakes

- ◆ Stand on left foot with right foot on ball of foot, upper body lifted and slightly back, bottom engaged, hands on hips.
- ◆ Lift right hip up by pressing into floor with right foot and straightening right knee slightly.
- ◆ Press right hip down, bending right knee and pushing left hip to side (hip shake).
- ◆ Repeat hip shake four times with right hip.
- ◆ Change feet, so that left foot is on ball of foot and repeat hip shakes four times with left hip.

start position

Repeat four times								
PATTERN	Right hip							
TIMING	& 1	& 2	& 3	& 4				

Repeat four times								
PATTERN	Left hip							
TIMING	& 5	& 6	& 7	& 8				

2 Add unscrewing the light bulb

- ◆ Twist both wrists at the same time as if unscrewing a light bulb.
- ◆ Repeat eight times.

Repeat eight times								
PATTERN	Twist	Twist	Twist	Twist	Twist	Twist	Twist	Twist
TIMING	**& 2**	& 2	& 3	& 4	& 5	& 6	& 7	& 8

wrist twisting action

&

wrist twisting action

1

x8

right hip up

&

right hip down

1

Shake and twist

- Perform hip shakes and unscrewing the light bulb movement at the same time, make your actions big and proud, add a shrug of the shoulder and really get into the feel of the movements and music.
- Repeat four times with each hip (right, right, right, right, left, left, left, left).

Repeat four times								
PATTERN	Right hip/both hands							
TIMING	**&**	**1**	&	2	&	3	&	4

Repeat four times								
PATTERN	Left hip/both hands							
TIMING	&	5	&	6	&	7	&	8

wrist twist

&

wrist twist

1

x8

Bollywood

Watch the video
Haynes.com/dancemanual

1 Hip shake, right and left

- Face front of room. Stand with weight on left foot, right foot on ball. Upper body lifted and slightly back, bottom engaged – left hand at side of head, finger tips backward, right hand on right hip.
- Eight hip shakes right hip.
- Change feet so left foot is on ball and right hand at side of head, fingers tips backward, left hand on left hip
- Eight hip shakes left hip.

Repeat eight times								
PATTERN	Right hip							
TIMING	& 1	& 2	& 3	& 4	& 5	& 6	& 7	& 8

Repeat eight times								
PATTERN	Left hip							
TIMING	& 2	& 2	& 3	& 4	& 5	& 6	& 7	& 8

start position

right hip shake

3 Add rain hands and stillness

- Raise both hands above head (or as high as possible). Separate out fingers.
- Flick hands outward three times, once where they are, once at shoulder level and once at waist level (rain hands).
- Hold this position (still).
- Repeat pattern.

Suggested music
....

- *Say Na Say Na,* from the movie *Bluffmaster* (2005)
- *Mil Gaye Jo Chhora-chhori,* from the movie *I Hate Luv Storys* (2010)

flick, arms up high
& 4

flick, shoulder level
& 2

2 Add four unscrewing the light bulb, high and at waist level

- Stand on both feet, or with right foot on ball, arms above head.
- Four unscrewing light bulbs.
- Lower arms to waist level.
- Four unscrewing light bulbs.

Repeat four times				
PATTERN	Twist wrists high			
TIMING	**& 3**	& 2	& 3	& 4

Repeat four times				
PATTERN	Twist wrists at waist			
TIMING	& 5	& 6	& 7	& 8

high　　　　　**waist level**

Repeat pattern								
PATTERN	High level	Shoulder level	Waist level	Stay still	High level	Shoulder level	Waist level	Stay still
TIMING	**& 4**	& 2	& 3	4	& 5	& 6	& 7	8

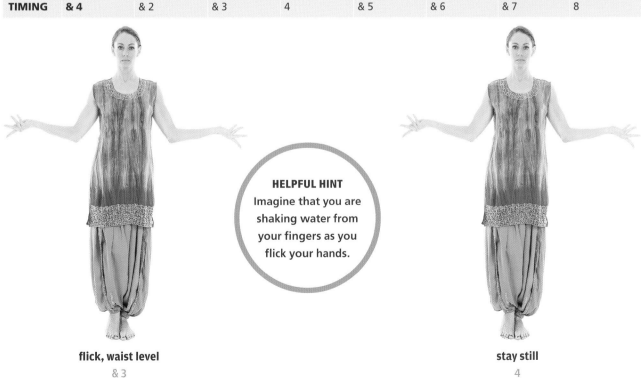

flick, waist level
& 3

HELPFUL HINT
Imagine that you are shaking water from your fingers as you flick your hands.

stay still
4

Bollywood *continued*

4 Add a turn anti-clockwise and a turn clockwise

- ◆ Stand on left foot with right foot on ball, left arm high and right hand to side at waist level, palms facing up.
- ◆ Press right foot into floor and swivel on heel of left foot turning to left (anti-clockwise), flick wrists.
- ◆ Repeat eight times making a complete turn.
- ◆ Change feet so weight is on right foot and right arm high.
- ◆ Repeat turning to right (clockwise).

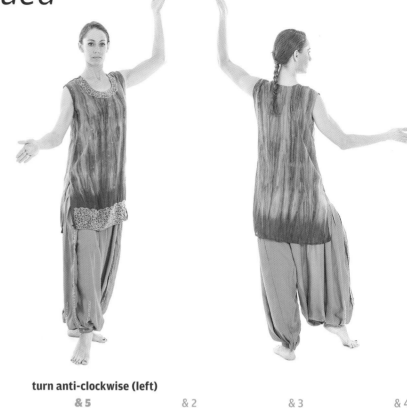

Repeat eight times							
PATTERN	Turn anti-clockwise (left)						
TIMING	**& 5**	& 2	& 3	& 4	& 5	& 6	& 7	& 8

Repeat eight times							
PATTERN	Turn Clockwise (right)						
TIMING	**& 6**	& 2	& 3	& 4	& 5	& 6	& 7	& 8

turn anti-clockwise (left)

    & 5   & 2   & 3   & 4

5 Add shimmy forward on lunge and shimmy backward

- ◆ Step forward on right foot, transfer weight over foot, bend knee (lunge), keep left foot on floor.
- ◆ Bring right shoulder forward (making left shoulder move backwards).
- ◆ Change so left shoulder forward, right shoulder backward.
- ◆ Change so right shoulder forward, left shoulder backward (shimmy forward).
- ◆ Transfer weight back on left foot, left knee bent, keep right foot on floor.
- ◆ Take right shoulder backward (making left shoulder move forward).
- ◆ Change so left shoulder backward right, shoulder forward.
- ◆ Change so right shoulder backward left, Shoulder forward (shimmy backward).
- ◆ Repeat shimmies forward and back four times.

Repeat four times							
PATTERN	Shimmy forward	Shimmy backward	Shimmy forward	Shimmy backward	Shimmy forward	Shimmy backward	Shimmy forward	Shimmy backward
TIMING	**7** & 2	3 & 4	5 & 6	7 & 8	**8** & 2	3 & 4	5 & 6	7 & 8

forward right shoulder

HELPFUL HINT
Join your feet together at the end of your turn clockwise, so it is easy to step onto your right foot for the lunges.

turn clockwise (right)

&5   &6   &7   &8   **&6** &2&3&4&5&6&7&8

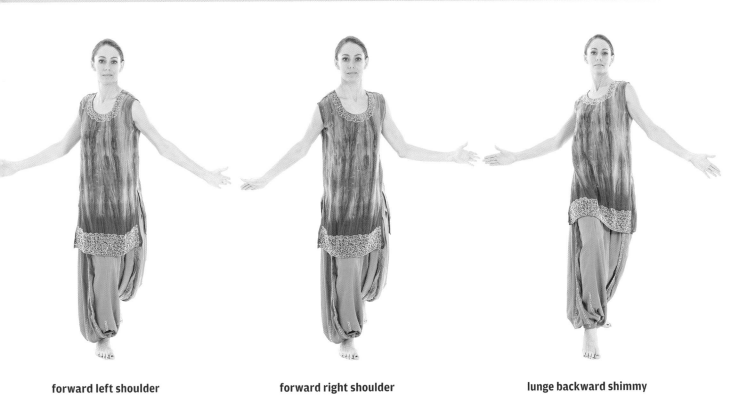

forward left shoulder   **forward right shoulder**   **lunge backward shimmy**

Improve your movements

- Work on the quality of your movements. Make them big and precise, working with the accents in the movement and music.
- Repeat the hip shakes at the same time as the light bulb movement.
- Add eight bop steps with right foot as you do the rain step arm movements.
- Stand on left foot with right foot on ball of foot (flat).
- Briefly step onto the toes of right foot (toe).
- Return to left foot flat on floor (flat).
- Repeat, (toe-flat) eight times with right foot as you do the rain step arms movements twice.

TECHNIQUE TIP
The transfer of weight is just for an instant. It is the same action as in a ball change in jazz or a balancé in ballet.

flick, arms up high / bop step right foot
& 4

flick, shoulder level / bop step right foot
& 2

Extra practise for co-ordination

◆ Pat your head with one hand and at the same time rub your tummy with the other.

◆ Walk across the room, clap your hands twice as you make each step (clapping twice as quickly as you are walking).

◆ Walk across the room, clapping once for every two steps you make (walking twice as quickly as you are clapping).

Bop step breakdown			
STEP ELEMENT	Stand on left foot with right foot on ball of foot	Step on toes of right foot	Return to left foot flat on floor
TIMING		&	1

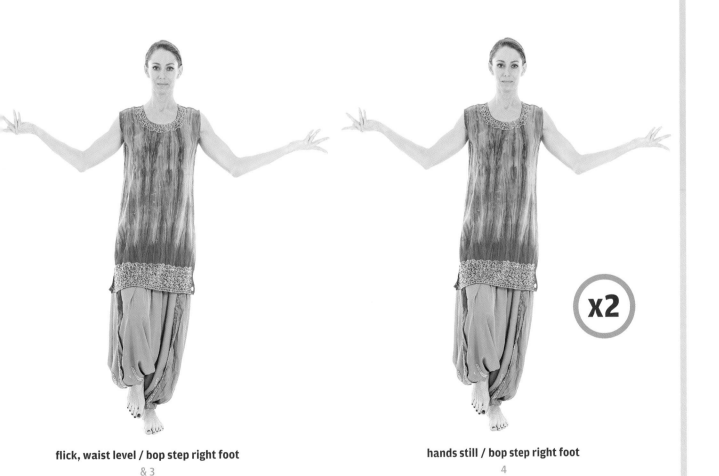

flick, waist level / bop step right foot

& 3

hands still / bop step right foot

4

x2

The Argentine tango

Argentine tango is one of the most popular and talked-about dance styles of the 21st century. It is all about improvisation, collaboration and interaction between two people and the music.

It began in the city of Buenos Aires and, like so many dance styles, was influenced by other cultures, in this case the mass immigration from Europe, Russia and Britain during the 19th and early 20th centuries. It is thought that the mainly male immigrants in Buenos Aires mixed with local *compadritos* (streetwise men) in the downtown venues where Milonga music (fast-paced polka combined with African rhythms) was played. Through such interactions the Tango developed and spread across the country and then the world, although the city of Buenos Aires remains the centre of Argentine tango.

The first tangos were played by small bands, which comprised of a harp, a flute and a violin. The bandoneon – originally from the German church – was embraced by the orchestras, replacing the flute. Its haunting sound has become central to Argentine tango music since the late 19th century.

In 1917 Carlos Gardel, a popular folk singer, recorded *Mi Noche Triste (My Sad Night)*. This was symbolic as the first recorded tango song and Gardel was credited with taking tango music to a mainstream audience. Several other singers, including Julio De Caro, went on to establish orchestras to show off their individual styles. Films starring Rudolph Valentino such as *The Four Horsemen of the Apocalypse* (1921) brought both him and the Argentine tango great fame during the 1920s and 1930s.

The period 1935–1950 is thought of as the 'Golden Age of Tango', as orchestras developed individual styles and gained followers for their particular music. In 1955, the military coup forced Argentine tango underground, but musicians and dancers continued to experiment. Astor Piazzolla embraced jazz and Western classical music, including elements in his compositions that in the 1970s took Argentine tango to a new audience across Europe.

Dancers also played their part. Carlos Copes and his partner María Nieves took the Argentine tango out of the social setting and onto the stage, playing a key part in starting a resurgence of interest across Europe in the 1980s. By the 1990s this popularity had spread rapidly in the UK and America. Broadway shows such as *Chicago* (1996) and films such as *The Tango Lesson* (1997) ensured that the Argentine tango's popularity continued to grow.

The tango and music

There are three rhythms within the Argentine tango. Alongside the tango there is the Vals rhythm (similar to a European waltz) and the Milonga rhythm, one of the earliest tango rhythms. Confusingly, a Milonga is also a dance rhythm as well as the name of a traditional social event!

The tango rhythm is the easiest to begin dancing with. If you like Argentine tango and want to really explore the dance style, you will need to become familiar with the different styles of music and the various orchestras to see which inspire you most to dance. The Argentine tango is about you, your connection with your partner and how you relate to the music. It relies more on your interpretation of the music than the steps and patterns themselves.

In recent years, performances on *Strictly Come Dancing* showing the newer choreographed theatre style have added to the interest. Vincent Simone and Flavia Cacace's shows in the West End go from strength to strength.

The tourist experience in Buenos Aires usually includes a 'Tango House' show. These are very entertaining and the performers are very skilled, but if you get the chance to attend a Milonga (a traditional social event), grab it with

both hands. A Milonga is divided into four sets or 'Tandas'. Each Tanda contains three or four dances of the same rhythm. Traditionally Milongas had many rules; today the atmosphere is more relaxed although it is important that the man asks the women to dance and the whole Tanda is danced with with the same partner. It is classed as impolite to only dance the first dance with someone and then change partner.

Argentine tango is an improvised dance. There is not a codified set of steps; more a process that partners take and together develop into their own style. In the 21st century, demand to adapt the dance style to the stage has led to a more choreographed and flamboyant style being developed. The World Championships (started in 2002) reflect this change in the two prizes:

1 The Choreography prize: choreographed pieces involving impressive lifts are staged for a theatre audience.
2 The Tango Salon or Social dance prize: this is performed on the floor and improvised. It involves improvising to tango music from three different orchestras and must not include anything that would impede another couple's dancing, such as lifts or high leg actions.

The Argentine tango class

Classes usually last an hour and teachers generally offer them at beginner and intermediate levels. It is ideal if you can take a partner, but many classes swap partners during the evening so don't worry about going to a class on your own.

The start of the class will always focus on making the connection between you and your partner and how you work together in the dance. The rest of the class will centre around the key elements of Argentine tango, such as walking, turning, stopping and interpreting the music. The teacher will do this through a mixture of teaching new steps and giving time for partners to improvise. As you improve and become more experienced you will spend more time on the subtlety of the different steps and do more improvisation. Most teachers encourage class members to swap partners, which is a good way to develop improvisation skills and stop you settling into predictable patterns.

Many teachers hold Milongas (special Tango social events). The early part of the evening is a class for those who are new to the style and is followed by a social occasion for the remainder of the evening. These evenings do not always follow the traditional Milonga rules.

Dress code

Most classes are informal and people wear styles they like and that suit them. The key is to have appropriate footwear. Neither men nor women need to invest in tango shoes for the first lesson, but it is important to have shoes that do not stick to the floor and that support your ankles. Do not wear trainers or any rubber-soled shoes, boots, sandals, or shoes with platforms or wedge heels, as this will be very frustrating, and make dancing difficult and unsafe for you.

As you improve, you will want to buy specialist shoes – these must fit well. Different designs and manufacturers suit different feet, so ask for advice when you are ready to buy a pair and/or try on a range of styles before you finally decide what to buy. Class teachers will often help you to find a pair of shoes that suit your feet as well as your budget.

In Argentine tango, the lady has her weight on the balls of her feet most of the time, so tango shoes are designed to support the instep more than in general ballroom shoes. Men's tango shoes are lighter than everyday shoes but are more stable than ballroom shoes. Good brands include Fabio Shoes, Salamanca and Flavella.

Starting out

Female

Skirts and dresses are ideal to wear, as they help to get the feel of the movement, but any lightweight clothing that is comfortable and doesn't restrict your movement is fine. A well-fitted shoe with a comfortable height heel is important. A heel is helpful to get the correct stance, but it must be at a height that you are used to wearing.

Male

Suit trousers or trousers from a soft fabric that do not restrict the leg movement are great. If all else fails, tracksuit bottoms are better than jeans. An everyday leather-soled shoe is fine to get you started.

REMEMBER
Personal hygiene is particularly important when dancing with a partner.

Stepping up

Female

As you progress, you will want to invest in a pair of specialist shoes to support your instep. You may also want to increase the height of the heel that you wear. Most dancers find a style of dress which suits them and that they are happy to wear.

Male

As you progress, you will want to invest in a pair of tango shoes that will enable you to slide and turn more easily. You may also want buy specialist tango trousers that give shaping to your moves when you dance.

Essential information

1 The embrace is key to dancing the Argentine tango successfully.

- Stand a few steps from your partner.
- Walk towards each other; stop, facing your partner with your bodies slightly apart.
- Both partners lean forward from the chest until you touch at the man's/leader's chest.
- Leader take follower's hand and follower places hand on leader's shoulder.
- Keep connected at the leader's chest, arms relaxed and elbows down.

2 The leader starts all movements from the chest and the follower starts all movements with the leg.

3 It is always important to remember that the Argentine tango is improvised, so to dance well both partners need to listen to each other's movements.

4 Listen to music by the orchestras suggested on page 142 so you become familiar with the sounds and rhythms.

page 142

Health benefits

Tango increases mobility, balance, stride length and core strength. The close physical and mental connection between the partners needed to improvise means that dancers lose themselves in the moment and become more relaxed. This connection can also improve the personal relationship between partners.

Fitness level:
Moderate

Complexity level:
High

TECHNIQUE TIP
The embrace is important so that the partners can communicate, responding to each other throughout the dance.

stand close

lean in

take embrace

Tango walk and posture

1 The tango walk

- Stand by yourself at one end of the room, feet together, arms loose by side, knees relaxed and weight slightly forward with chest up and forward.
- Transfer weight to right foot.
- Leading from your chest, step forward left foot, leaving right foot behind.
- Drag right foot forward to meet left foot (collect), keep weight on left foot.
- Step through with right foot for second step.
- Drag left foot forward to meet right foot (collect), keep weight on right foot.
- Repeat as many times as you can across the room.
- Try to relax and feel the timing in the music.

> ### Suggested music
>
> - Any tango rhythm by these orchestras
> - Hotel Victoria Orchestra: Francisco Canaro
> - Bahía Blanca Orchestra: Carlos Di Sarli
> - La Cumparsita Orchestra: Juan D'Arienzo

weight right foot

step forward left foot

1

2 Repeat, moving backward

- Stand by yourself at one end of the room, feet together arms loose by side, knees relaxed and weight slightly forward.
- Transfer weight to left foot.
- Reach back with right foot, toe leading.
- Step onto ball of right foot and roll through foot to put heel down.
- Bring left foot back to meet right foot (collect), keep weight forward and over right foot (position zero).
- Reach back with left foot for second step.
- Drag right foot forward to meet left foot (collect), keep weight on left foot (position zero).
- Repeat as many times as you can across the room.
- Try to relax and feel the flow of the walk.

> **HELPFUL HINT**
> It's good to practise on your own before joining with a partner.

weight left foot

reach back right foot

1

collect	step through right foot	collect
2 3 4	5 6 7	8

collect	reach back left foot	collect
2 3 4	5 6 7	8

Practice task 2
Changing weight in the embrace

1 Changing weight in the embrace

- Stand in basic embrace.
- Keep point of contact at leader's chest.
- Leader initiating movement from chest, transfer most of weight onto right foot so that left foot is slightly off the floor.
- *Follower responding to the movement by leader, transfer most weight onto left foot so that right foot is slightly off the floor.*
- Repeat, changing weight eight times, leader indicate when changes happen.

TECHNIQUE TIP
Follower concentrate on your following role – don't try to lead!

embrace
embrace

position zero (right foot)
position zero (left foot)

Practice task 3
Walks with your partner

- Stand in basic embrace. Keep the point of contact at the leader's chest.
- Leader transfer weight to right foot.
  (Follower transfer weight to left foot.)
- Leader step forward with left foot, leading the movement from chest.
  (Follower feel the movement start in the chest and when the leader steps forward start reply with a step backward with right foot.)
- Both collect foot to zero position.
- Repeat the walk four times.
- Change weight in this position (up to four times).
- Repeat the steps and changes of weight again as many times as you can.
- Put on a piece of music and get lost in the atmosphere.

prepare by transferring weight to right foot
prepare by transferring weight to left foot

step forward left foot
step backward right foot

repeat transferring weight
repeat transferring weight

A different way

Try the task in different ways

◆ Just with the torsos touching, so the leader really needs to initiate the movement from the chest and the follower senses that movement.

◆ Make your transfers of weight smaller and smaller so that your weights shifts but your feet do not leave the floor.

◆ With the follower closing their eyes but NOT the leader.

TECHNIQUE TIP
Each step takes one count. Try and keep the subtlety of the movement now that you are moving faster.

complete step
complete step

x4

collect to zero position
collect to zero position

x4
MAX

transfer weight
transfer weight

HELPFUL HINT
If you transfer weight an odd number of times, you will use your other leg for the next step.

REMEMBER
Followers, be gentle with the leader as they have a lot of thinking to do as well as moving – be patient!

Argentine tango

Watch the video
Haynes.com/dancemanual

1 Step 1 – walk and collect

- Leader stand on left side of room.
  (Follower stand on right side of room.)
  Face each other.
- Move into the basic embrace. Keep the point of contact at the leader's chest.
- Leader transfer weight to left foot.
  (Follower transfer weight to right foot.)
- Leader step backward right foot.
  (Follower step forward left foot.)
- Collect to zero position, leader weight on right foot.
  (Collect, follower weight on left foot.)

TECHNIQUE TIP
This sequence is known as the basic step in six and is a foundation of the Argentine tango.

embrace
embrace

step backward right foot
step forward left foot
1

2 Step 2 – Step to the side and collect

- Leader step side left foot.
  (Follower step side right foot.)
- Collect to zero position, leader weight on left foot.
  (Collect, follower weight on right foot.)

REMEMBER
The leader starts every step from their chest.

step side left foot
step side right foot
2

transfer weight
transfer weight

collect
collect

HELPFUL HINT
The basic step in six makes a box pattern on the floor. Remember the leader takes the first step backward and the follower takes the first step forward.

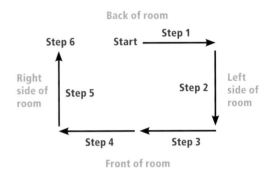

Back of room

Step 6 | Start | Step 1

Right side of room | Step 5 | | Step 2 | Left side of room

Step 4 | Step 3

Front of room

transfer weight
transfer weight

collect
collect

Suggested music

◆ *El Cholo*, Orchestra Tipica Victor (1929)

---

3 **Step 3 – Walk and collect**

◆ Leader step forward right foot.
(*Follower step backward left foot.*)

◆ Collect, leader weight right foot.
(*Collect, follower weight left foot.*)

HELPFUL HINT
To avoid kicking the follower, leader keep right foot across own body on forward step.

step forward right foot
step backward left foot
3

transfer weight
transfer weight

collect
collect

Argentine tango *continued*

4 Step 4 – Walk and collect:

- Leader step forward left foot.
  (Follower step backward right foot.)
- Collect, leader weight left foot.
  (Collect, follower weight right foot.)

step forward left foot
step backward right foot
4

transfer weight
transfer weight

5 Step 5 – Step to side and collect:

- Leader step side right foot.
  (Follower step side left foot.)
- Collect, leader weight right foot.
  (Collect, follower weight on left foot.)

step side right foot
step side left foot
5

transfer weight
transfer weight

collect
collect

Improvise

◆ Improvise around the basic step in six. Add some changes of weight in between the individual steps. Do not discuss the changes. Leaders, tell your partner what to do by leading from the chest and followers, listen and feel what the leader wants you to do next. Followers, remember that you choose the timing at which you respond to the leader's request!

collect
collect

6 Step 6 – Change weight:

◆ Leader changes weight to left foot. *(Follower changes weight to right foot.)*

◆ Keep repeating the sequence.

change weight left foot
change weight right foot

6

Belly dance

The popularity of belly dancing continues to rise in the UK, Europe and America. Belly dancing is a term used in Western cultures for a collection of dance styles originating from Egypt, Lebanon, Turkey and North Africa, where dance traditionally is accepted as both a social and an art form.

Throughout Upper Egypt, the Nile Delta and in the big cities, the dance is performed at weddings, birthdays and circumcisions – in fact at almost any kind of celebration! Guests take it in turns to get up and entertain each other before, after and sometimes during the performance of the hired professional dancers. Styles in the UK and America usually have roots in dance from Egypt.

In Arab countries the women and men of the society lead quite separately structured lives. Women dance in their own homes for each other, or as individuals dancing within a group, using dance as a form of individual expression. Men do dance, but this is often following a performance by a professional dancer in a more public arena, such as at a wedding. There are many lively debates about the development of this dance form, especially as it is experienced in Western cultures! Whatever the origins and development routes, it now offers a central plank to tourists' experiences in Egypt and the opportunity for women to dance together regularly in many countries across the world.

In Egypt the dance is a subtle mix of spinal movement, arm gesture, hip and chest movements, performed in an easy and leisurely style from a grounded stance. There are no globally recognised names for the movements and no consensus as to the precise number of families or groups of movements, although they are generally grouped into three broad categories:

1 Percussive movements: staccato movements, usually of the hips but also with the shoulders and ribcage, used to punctuate the music or accent a beat.
2 Fluid movements: flowing, sinuous movements showing the suppleness of the body, used to interpret melody or lyrical sections in the music.
3 Shimmies, shivers and vibrations: fast, small movements of the hips or ribcage that look like one continuous movement

Above: Fifi Abdou is still performing at 63.

Belly dancing is an improvised dance style, and whether someone is dancing socially or as a paid performer, the dancers will use the same steps. The professional dancer may have a bigger repertoire of movements, but they will all come from the three groups mentioned above. What is important is how a dancer makes the moves 'their own', and how they relate to the audience, making them feel part of the performance. People go to watch professional performers because of their style and personality, the way they interpret the subtle nuances in the music and their overall approach to the dance – not to see increasingly complex steps and patterns. This means people can still enjoy to dance as they get older. Fifi Abdou and Nagwa Fouad remain leading performers although they are now both over 60.

As a social dance form it is easy for women to learn a few steps and gain from the empowering nature of the style. This makes it a popular choice for women of all ages and sizes. However, to gain the strength, control and subtly to perform the movements well takes longer and is much harder than you might think.

In the UK, Europe and America the dance style is called by various names including Belly dancing, Arabic dance, Oriental dance or Raqs Sharqi. This can be confusing, but in reality the only difference to the classes is in the name.

Belly dance and music

Traditionally the music is repetitive with subtle changes of key and rhythm working within a strict framework. Music played today is a fusion of traditional folk and baladi (urban) traditions, with elements from African, Arab, Turkish and Western music. The dancer improvises steps following the structure of the music, each family of steps having a particular role with the music.

The dance is usually undertaken with a live band, with the dancer and musicians taking cues from each other, developing a rapport between each other and the audience, and adding to the individual style of the dancer. Sometimes dancers use 'sagat' (brass castanets) when they dance, adding another layer of interaction.

The belly dance class

Classes are usually women only, last for about an hour and have a relaxed and informal atmosphere. Some teachers still lead classes with participants standing in straight lines, although most – at least for the start of the class – work in a circle emphasising the community and social aspects of the style.

The precise structure of classes will vary according to the teacher, but all start with a warm-up and include a section of learning or practising family groups of steps (percussive movements, fluid movements and shimmies, etc.). Some class teachers like to choreograph dances; others emphasise the individual nature of the style and give participants lots of choice about the steps used.

Most teachers now use a mixture of music and any set choreographies often move away from the strict frameworks set by the traditional music. There is usually an improvisation or 'free' section of the class where you can develop your own style and experiment with interpreting the music. A typical way this happens is as

a group dance, which starts with everyone standing in a circle. Individuals enter the circle and perform a short improvised dance while other class members remain in the circle still dancing. This can be daunting to begin with, but give it a go – even if you only do a few movements, you will find it empowering. The teacher will always lead a cool-down at the end of the class.

Some teachers grade their classes into beginner, intermediate and advanced, but you may find yourself in a general class alongside experienced dancers. The improvised and interactive nature of this dance style means that it can work well in this format, providing the opportunity to look and learn from others as you develop your own style.

Many local areas hold 'Haflas' (party or social gathering), where dance groups meet together to share dancing and Middle Eastern food. These are a chance to dress up and show your moves on the dance floor, either as a solo or often as part of a group dance.

Dress code

Belly dance classes offer a chance to dress in bright colours, wear jewellery and flaunt some flesh – if you want to! People usually become more adventurous as they become familiar with the dance style and see the range of costumes worn by other class members. Scarves or coin belts are used around the hips to increase awareness of this important area and to give a feeling of being grounded.

Starting out

Female
A long full skirt or harem pants with a T-shirt or cropped top and a light shawl or scarf tied around the hips are ideal. However, a fitted top with leggings and a big scarf around your hips is all that is needed to get you started. Bare feet, or soft-soled shoes that allow your feet to flex and stretch are fine.

Stepping up

Female
What you wear as you progress may depend on other class members and the group as a whole. Investing in a coin belt will liven up any outfit and help with the grounded stance.

Essential information

1 The basic posture is a grounded, relaxed, natural stance with the upper body lifted and bottom muscles engaged.

2 The arms are used to frame the movement and draw attention to different parts of the body.

3 Veils are often used in dances.

4 Moving different parts of your body independently is important in belly dancing. Gently shake your body from head to toe to relax it. Try doing this to a piece of belly dancing music, stopping your movements with the accents in the music – enjoy and let yourself go!

Health benefits

Many of the moves involve isolations, which improve the flexibility and strength of the torso. The social nature and womanly celebration of the form creates a real sense of well-being.

Fitness level:
Low

Complexity level:
Low/Moderate

WARNING
Belly dance works your knees, hips and the centre of the body intensively, so take care of these areas. If you find any of the movements painful, stop dancing. When you re-start, make your movements smaller.

Snake arms

1 Lift right arm and left arm

- Stand in basic stance.
- Lift right arm up side to shoulder level, imagine you are holding a large beach ball.
- Imagine releasing the ball, let elbow lead arm back to original position.
- Repeat four times right arm.
- Repeat four times left arm.

start position   right arm up

2 Add moving both arms together

- Lift right arm up side to shoulder level, imagine you are holding a large beach ball.
- Imagine releasing the ball, let elbow lead right arm back to original position.
- As right arm starts to lower, lift left arm reaching shoulder level as right arm reaches original position.
- Repeat this wave action four times.

HELPFUL HINT
Don't worry about counts, just get the feel of the movement.

start position   right arm up

right arm down

right arm down and left arm up

Hip lifts and hip drops

1 Eight hip lifts

- Stand in natural stance, upper body lifted, bottom engaged – knees slightly bent and arms to the side.
- Straighten right leg, do not lock knee or push hip to side (right hip lift).
- Straighten left leg, do not lock knee or push hip to side (left hip lift), bend right knee as left leg straightens.
- Repeat eight times (right, left, right, left, right, left, right, left).

HELPFUL HINT
When you straighten your right leg you will feel your right side shorten.

start position

hip lift right

1

2 Add eight hip drops

- Step onto right foot, pressing into floor, bending knee to drop right hip (right hip drop).
- Step onto left foot, pressing into floor, bending knee to drop left hip (left hip drop).
- Repeat eight times (right, left, right, left, right, left, right, left).

TECHNIQUE TIP
Keep your hips as straight as possible when you do hip lifts and hip drops; try not to push your hip to the side, or twist your body.

start position

hip drop right

1

hip lift left

2

hip lift right

3

HELPFUL HINT
Don't worry if one side of
your body makes bigger
movements than the other
– it just means one side
is stronger. This is a good
way to strengthen your
weaker side.

x4

hip drop left

2

Something harder
Faster movements

◆ Repeat the task, making your movements faster.
See how fast you can go while still keeping the
preciseness of each movement.

Belly dancing sequence

Watch the video
Haynes.com/dancemanual

1 Snake arms facing back and front left corner

◆ Stand in centre of room facing back of room.

◆ Snake arms to side for the first phrase of the music (probably two sets).

◆ Turn to face left corner, front of room, right foot on ball of foot.

◆ Continue snake arms at front of body.

Suggested music

◆ *Sultans of the Dance, Anadolu Atesi*

HELPFUL HINT
The music used in the video doesn't have a slow section at the start.

snake arms facing back of room

2 Add four steps across with a hip lift

◆ Place right foot flat on floor, transfer weight onto foot facing left front corner of room.

◆ Point left foot to side, lift left hip face front of room.

◆ Step across left foot, foot flat on floor, in front of right foot.

◆ Point right foot to side, lift right hip.

◆ Step across right foot, foot flat on floor, in front left foot.

◆ Point left foot side, lift left hip.

◆ Step across left foot, foot flat on floor, in front right foot.

◆ Bring right foot to left foot into basic stance.

Step across right foot

lift left hip

PATTERN	Step across right foot	Lift left hip	Step across left foot	Lift right hip	Step across right foot	Lift left hip	Step across left foot	Step into basic stance
TIMING	1	2	3	4	5	6	7	8

snake arms facing diagonal

step left foot across front

REMEMBER
Play with your audience, whether they are other dancers or people sitting watching.

lift right hip

Belly dancing sequence *continued*

3 Add two slow hip figures of eight and two faster

◆ Transfer weight to right side of feet, taking hips to right side, keeping upper body still.

◆ Transfer weight towards toes (as if doing an anticlockwise circle) taking right hip towards right corner, front of room.

◆ Transfer weight diagonally back across feet, taking hips towards the left corner, back of room.

◆ Transfer weight towards toes (as if doing a clockwise circle) taking left hip towards left corner, front of room.

◆ Transfer weight diagonally back across feet taking hips towards right corner, back of room.

◆ Repeat making another slow hip figure of eight, starting from this position.

◆ Make two more figures of eight taking four counts for each.

hips side right

hips twist front right corner

hips side right

hips twist front right corner

> **WARNING**
> Keep your movements small so that you move safely from your hips. You can make them bigger as you gain strength and flexibility.

> **TECHNIQUE TIP**
> Let your arms move naturally with the movements, or keep them out to the side.

PATTERN	Figure of 8 to right	Figure of 8 to right	Figure of 8 to right	Figure of 8 to right
TIMING	2 2 3 4 5 6 7 8	3 2 3 4 5 6 7 8	4 2 3 4	5 6 7 8

hips back diagonally

hips twist front left corner

hips back diagonally

hips back diagonally

hips twist front left corner

hips back diagonally

HELPFUL HINT
Imagine tracing
this shape

on the floor with
your hips.

Belly dancing sequence *continued*

4 **Add eight hip drops right hip and eight hip drops left hip**

- Stand on left foot, place right foot on ball facing left corner, front of room, left hand at the side of head, finger tips backward just above ear. right arm to side.
- Eight right hip drops.
- Change position to face right corner, front of room, stand on right foot, left foot on ball of foot, right hand at the side of head, finger tips backwards just above ear, left arm to side.
- Eight left hip drops.

x8

right hip drop

1

5 **Add four hip drops turning to face the back of the room and a shimmy**

- Step on left foot pressing into floor to drop hip.
- Step on right foot (knee slightly bent) pushing into the floor to drop right hip.
- Repeat hip drops until you face the back of the room.
- Continue hip drops raising arms above head into high 'v'.
- Bend knees less and change legs more quickly to increase the speed of hip drops (shimmy).
- Turn and repeat the sequence from the cross steps and hip lift.

hip drops turning to face back of room

x8

left hip drop

Improvise

◆ Put on one of the suggested pieces of music on page 157, or a piece of your own choice, and combine any of the steps that you have learned as you improvise to the music. Remember what you know about which types of steps go with different types of music.

HELPFUL HINT
Listen to the music several times before you start so that you are familiar with its rhythms and timing.

raise arms and shimmy to finish

Burlesque

Burlesque continues to rise in popularity with nearly 50 shows a week and an increasing number of classes for people to attend. In Europe, burlesque was traditionally a term used to describe any bawdy satirical performance.

In the latter part of the 19th century, burlesque shows were popular and thrived in music halls across the UK, and vaudeville theatres and burlesque houses in the USA. The performances blended song and dance with ribald humour, poking fun at art and music or making social comment. Gradually the shows, in America, became more about leggy, under-dressed dancers, although they kept a sense of fun.

There were strict laws governing nudity and the shows were quite tame. Lydia Thompson and The British Blondes are credited with having the first burlesque hit on Broadway with *Ixion* (1868). It was considered outrageous but glamorous; witty women covered in little more than body stockings teasing their audience proved to be an irresistible combination and burlesque became increasing popular.

By the early 20th century burlesque houses were gaining a dubious reputation and vaudeville stars tried to divorce themselves from burlesque performances. However, in reality many of them started and finished their careers performing in burlesque houses and successful film stars such as Mae West also began their careers as burlesque entertainers. In the 1920s frank sexual content had come to define burlesque. With the decline of the burlesque houses and music halls, burlesque went underground and it was at this time that it really gained the reputation of being striptease. Even so, burlesque remained more about the 'tease' than the 'strip', with glamour and glitz central to the performances.

Burlesque acts such as Gypsy Rose Lee and Sally Rand gained mainstream appeal starring in films. Gypsy Rose Lee was admired as much for the witty and intelligent banter that she used in her performances as she was for the taking off of her clothes (or as many as the law would allow). Sally Rand is most famous for her dances using giant ostrich feathers and a large transparent bubble. Glamour and glitz were central to the performances.

Burlesque disappeared almost completely by the 1950s, as it was seen as too raunchy for mainstream entertainment and too tame to compete with the more overt strip clubs. Society, however, remained mesmerised by burlesque, and the film *The Night They Raided Minsky's* (1968) and the Broadway hit *Sugar*

Babies (1979) reminded the public of the glamour, mystique and infamy that comes with burlesque.

Since the 1990s burlesque has once again increased in popularity. Often called New Burlesque, a generation of performers now use both satire and American pin-up girl styles in their performances. The style remains sexy rather than sexual and true to burlesque history, the performers do not take themselves too seriously. The glamour and glitz of a performance remains key for modern performers

Burlesque and music

Burlesque dancers can use any type of music. New Orleans jazz is popular, as it can evoke the feel of smoky bars and something not quite proper! Whatever the genre of music used it is always a big and powerful song befitting the glitz and showiness of burlesque. The dancer will often relate to the lyrics of a song as well as the beat, to give direction to the dance.

such as Dita Von Teese, who revels in the fun of burlesque, undertaking outrageous stunts such as performing just wearing diamonds or in a giant martini glass. Props and style galore remain the rule!

Burlesque has been given a 21st century makeover with a supper club scene, monthly battles to find the next Burlesque Idol, a range of shows in capital cities around the world and multiple touring productions. Many of these performances encourage the audience to dress up, adding to the sense of fun. There are several strong virtual networks such as the Ministry of Burlesque and Retro Tease Network that connect burlesque fans with each other and give news about events and activities.

The burlesque class

The number of burlesque classes is increasing all of the time. They usually last about an hour and are popular with women of all ages. The nature of the dance leads to a relaxed atmosphere and a good group spirit. Although some teachers divide their groups into beginner and more advanced, most classes have dancers with different levels of experience. This is perfect for the dance style, as a few people dancing with confidence can really help you let go when you are new to a class. Burlesque is about confidence and having fun, so if you attend a class, go along with a can-do attitude and enter into the spirit.

Classes begin with a warm-up designed to strengthen the body and improve flexibility. This is followed by a number of tasks and sequences developing the clean lines and confident posture needed for the style. Not to mention how to strut in high heels! Sometimes this section looks at 'the reveal' – how to take off gloves, a belt or how to use a prop such as a boa or fan. Classes also focus on developing performance skills to help members to find their inner burlesque dancer and develop their individual style. The last section of the class is a routine built up over a number of weeks, so that class members can try out their performance skills. All classes will finish with a cool-down.

Some teachers arrange performances between groups. This is a chance to show your moves to a bigger audience, but it will always be an option and not obligatory. Other teachers arrange trips to burlesque venues and cabaret nights.

Dress code

Anything goes, from simple and comfortable clothes to feathers, sequins and plenty of glitz! Most classes will have a mixture of some people who dress up in a corset and others who wear leggings and a T-shirt. People generally become more adventurous as they become familiar with the dance style and as dressing up is part of the attraction of burlesque, so most people find themselves gradually buying clothes and props.

As with many dance styles, shoes are important, but a sturdy, well-fitted heeled shoe will be good to start. A heel of about 5cm (2in) is ideal and lower is fine, especially if you are not used to wearing high heels. Ballroom shoes work well because they are lighter than everyday shoes, or an Argentine tango shoe, which has a more solid base, would be suitable.

Props such as fans, boas and gloves are always fun and often used in classes. Many teachers will provide these items, especially for people who are new to the class.

Starting out

Female

Comfortable clothing, such as a T-shirt and leggings, are fine to get you started. You will need a pair of well-fitted shoes with a sturdy heel that you feel safe to move in.

Stepping up

Female

What you wear as you progress may depend on other class members and the group as a whole. Most people invest in a pair of ballroom shoes and you may want to start wearing more of a costume, such as a basque. Buying your own props and adornments (such as gloves, hat or a fan) is a good way to start developing your wardrobe.

Essential information

1 It is important to have a basic stance that exudes confidence. Stand tall, head up, chin out, chest forward and bottom out, making an arch in your back.

2 Burlesque is about attitude, so be bold and cheeky.

Health benefits

Burlesque improves your core strength and your posture, but its main benefit is making you feel proud of your body and confident in yourself. This increased confidence and acceptance gives a great sense of well-being.

Fitness level:
Low

Complexity level:
Low

WARNING
Do not wear shoes with higher heels than you are used to wearing. It is better to start with a lower heel and be safe.

3 Burlesque dancers often use adornments such as boas, gloves and fans to add a feeling of glamour and to tease the audience.

Struts and poses

1 Four struts

- Stand in basic stance, facing right corner, front of room, with hands on hips.
- Pick up right foot, a bit like a horse prancing.
- Step on right foot.
- Repeat (right, left, right, left).

HELPFUL HINT
Use a feather boa or long scarf over your shoulders to help you maintain the upright and proud posture.

Suggested music
....

- *Express*, Christine Aguilera
- *Big Spender*, Shirley Bassey
- *Harlem Nocturne*, Johnny Otis

start position

pick up right foot
1

2 Add four different poses

- Stand in confident position.
- Bend both knees slightly.
- Raise right arm, bend right knee a bit further (Pose 1).
- Straighten left leg, cross arms so that hands touch opposite shoulder (or as close as you can get them) (Pose 2).
- Step onto right foot, turn to right, put most of weight onto right foot, place left foot on toe, bend both knees.
- Cross right arm over left arm, place fingertips of both hands on left knee (Pose 3).
- Straighten both legs, place hands on lower back.
- Push bottom out and chest forward creating an arch in back (Pose 4).
- Eight walks on the spot.

TECHNIQUE TIP
Strut and pose around the room, making your movements big and bold. Use your own poses, not just the ones included in this task.

HELPFUL HINT
Use the eight steps on the spot to change direction before you repeat the 4 struts.

start position

PATTERN	4 struts	Pose 1	Pose 2	Pose 3	Pose 4	8 walks on the spot
TIMING	**1** 2 3 4 5 6 7 8	**2** 2 3 4	5 6 7 8	**3** 2 3 4	5 6 7 8	**4** 2 3 4 5 6 7 8

step right foot
2

pick up left foot
3

step left foot
4

x2

Remember

- ◆ Do the general warm-ups before tackling this section.
- ◆ Practise each section of the practice tasks separately before joining it onto another section.
- ◆ Repeat the whole task several times when you have joined all of the sections together.
- ◆ Refresh your memory of the abbreviations by looking at the introduction again.

pose 1
2234

pose 2
5678

pose 3
3234

pose 4
5678

Arm movements and shoulder circles

1 Reach right arm to side and then place on left shoulder

◆ Stand in confident position facing front of room. Stand on left leg, right knee bent, some weight on ball of foot, keep left hand on hip all of the time.

◆ Reach right arm to side, look along arm into distance.

◆ Bend right arm at elbow.

◆ Draw right elbow to waist.

◆ Place right hand on left shoulder (or as close as you can get it), bring right shoulder slightly forward, look over it.

◆ Draw right hand across body, place on right hip, turn to face left corner, front of room. Look over right shoulder.

◆ Hold pose.

start position

right arm side

1 2

2 Add two right shoulder circles and change to pose facing right corner, front of room

◆ Circle right shoulder backward, look over shoulder.

◆ Repeat.

◆ Step on right foot to face front of room.

◆ Close left leg to right leg, left knee bent, some weight on ball of foot.

◆ Repeat whole sequence using left arm, keep right hand on hip all of the time.

REMEMBER
When you repeat the task, you will need to turn to face the front right corner of the room to 'show off' your shoulder circles.

x2

hands on hips

circle right shoulder

2 2 3 4 5 6 7 8

right arm on left shoulder

3 4

both hands on hip and pose

5 6 7 8

TECHNIQUE TIP
Although the movements are easy, doing them slowly and strongly take strength and confidence.

Something harder

Use your hips

◆ Repeat the task but circle hips instead of shoulder.
◆ Lift right hip and circle it backward.
◆ Let left shoulder come forward and right shoulder backward as you make the circle.
◆ Repeat four times with right hip and then repeat four times with left hip.

TECHNIQUE TIP
Keep your head up and make the movement fill the music.

HELPFUL HINT
The circle will be quite small.

right hip circle

x4

left shoulder forward

Burlesque sequence

Watch the video
Haynes.com/dancemanual

1 High 'V' with arms and chest cross

- Stand tall, right foot on ball of foot, feet together, hands on hips, face front.
- Walk on the spot as you do foot movements (get into the feel for the music).
- Extend right arm high, hold the boa, look at hand.
- Raise left arm to make a high 'V'.
- Bring right arm across chest, rest hand on left shoulder, bring right shoulder slightly forward.
- Bring left arm across chest, rest hand on right shoulder and left shoulder slightly forward.

HELPFUL HINT
If you find walking on the spot is stressful, just work on the arm movements first and add the feet later.

start position

raise right arm
1

2 Add side reaches with arms

- Extend right arm to side at shoulder level, look along right arm into distance.
- Leave arm there.
- Extend left arm to side at shoulder level, look along left arm into distance.

HELPFUL HINT
You can use a long scarf instead of a feather boa.

extend right arm
5 6

TECHNIQUE TIP
Keep hold of
your boa if
you can.

raise left arm
2

cross right arm
3

cross left arm
4

extend left arm
7 8

HELPFUL HINT
If you are walking
on the spot, your feet
may be different to
the pictures.

Suggested music

◆ *Fever*, Peggy Lee
◆ *Feeling Good*, Michael Bublé

Burlesque sequence *continued*

3 Four struts to the side and stroke right leg and left leg

- Four struts, starting with right foot.
- Bring arms across chest as you strut.
- Point right foot to side.
- Stroke right hand up right leg to a high 'v' position.
- Bring arms across chest.
- Repeat moving to the left starting the struts with left foot.

REMEMBER
Do your preparation
lift of the leg for
the strut.

start position

PATTERN	Struts right, left, right, left	Point right foot side	High 'v' arm	Struts left, right, left, right	Point left foot side	High 'v' left arm
TIMING	**2** 2 3 4	5	6 7 8	**3** 2 3 4	5	6 7 8

4 Add four hip circles right, left

- Place hands on hips and change weight to stand on left leg, right foot on ball of foot facing left corner, front of room.
- Lift right hip and make four hip circles backward.
- Turn shoulders so that left shoulder comes forward and right shoulder backward as you finish each circle.
- Change weight so left foot is on ball, repeat four times with left hip.

hands on hips

right hip circles backward
4 2 3 4 5 6 7

x4

end struts feet together

point right foot side

take right arm to high 'v'

change direction

8

left hip circles backward

5 2 3 4 5 6 7 8

TECHNIQUE TIP
Hold onto your
core/tummy
muscles to help
you balance.

x4

Burlesque sequence *continued*

5 Add a slow turn with arms crossed over chest

- ◆ Cross right foot over left foot, cross left arm over right arm, rest hands on shoulders.
- ◆ Slow turn left (anticlockwise).
- ◆ Finish with weight on right foot.

> **WARNING**
> Only lean forward as far as you feel safe and comfortable to; you could topple over if you go too far. Reaching to your thigh or knee with style is very effective.

cross right foot over left foot cross arms over chest

6   2

6 Add point forward and stroke

- ◆ Point left foot forward.
- ◆ Lean your upper body over, stroke up leg with both hands.
- ◆ Gather hands at neck and raise arms into high 'v'.

point left foot and lean forward   **stroke up body**   **gather hands**

5   6   7

slowly turn
3

high 'V'
8

finish with weight on right foot
4

Something harder
Improvise

◆ Relax more into the feel of the music and improvise a few moves to add to the dance.
◆ Make a turn (instead of the struts) before the leg stroke.
◆ Let go of the boa and circle your wrist as well as the hips.

TECHNIQUE TIP
If you are making any turns, you will need to hold onto your core (tummy muscles) to keep your balance.

Adapting dance for sitting on a chair

Most dance styles can be adapted so that you can still capture the joy of dancing and feel the essence of each style whilst sitting on a chair.

You may want to do this when you need to lessen the stress on lower body joints, or balance is an issue, such as when you are:

◆ recovering from illness or an operation;
◆ managing lower body injuries;
◆ slowing down a bit with age;
◆ coping with weight issues that make load-bearing exercise difficult;
◆ or maybe you haven't exercised for years and just want a bit of fun to get you started!

If you have elderly parents, why not join them in experimenting with some of the dance styles in this book whilst sitting in a chair? Choose a dance style that they enjoyed in the past, or start with a piece of music that has special memories for them. As well as gaining the benefits of dancing, the music may spark memories of when they were young and you might get to hear some tales from their past, or it could create the opportunity to share memories from when you were both younger.

Whatever your reason for dancing whilst sitting on a chair, remember to start gently and increase your range of movement and the number of times that you repeat the task or sequence gradually. You will gain strength and flexibility as well as having fun, but it will take time.

Essential information

1 Movements with limbs are easier to adapt than whole body movements.

2 Travelling steps are hard to adapt, particularly for those who would need the support of a chair.

3 The general strength and flexibility of the person on the chair will influence the steps and patterns that can be made.

4 Remember the key characteristics of the style you are using – these will give the flavour to any steps that you adapt.

5 Big, comfortable armchairs limit the range of movements that can be done. It is better to use a firmer chair, preferably without arms.

6 Beware of leaning too far forward or to the sides, as you could easily lose your balance.

7 Twisting from the hips takes a lot of strength.

8 Use music as a motivator.

9 Use props that add to the feel of the dance, e.g. a feather boa for Burlesque or 'button taps' for tap (see helpful hint page 189).

10 Combining different rhythms, such as a Bop step and Rain step in a Bollywood sequence, will get the brain working as well as the body. Experiment – give it a go!

TECHNIQUE TIP
Choose a chair that allows you to keep your knees at 90° and your feet flat on the floor. Use a sturdy chair, not a folding or rolling chair, and sit up tall.

Breathing, head turns and tilts

1 Simple breathing

- Sit on a sturdy chair, cross arms and touch ribs.
- Breathe in and out in four counts – feel your ribs move in and out (breath naturally, don't over-concentrate).
- Repeat.

breathing arms crossed on ribs

2 Add head turns

- Turn head right.
- Return centre.
- Turn head left.
- Return centre.
- Repeat twice (right, centre, left, centre, right, centre, left, centre).

turn right

Repeat twice				
PATTERN	Breathe in	Breathe out	Breathe in	Breathe out
TIMING	**1** 2 3 4	5 6 7 8	**2** 2 3 4	5 6 7 8

3 Add head tilts

- Place hands on shoulders to make sure they don't rise up.
- Tilt head right.
- Return centre.
- Tilt head left.
- Return centre.
- Repeat twice (right, centre, left, centre, right, centre, left, centre).

HELPFUL HINT
The number of counts for the head turns and tilts are different, so you will need to really think about how you count the task.

start position

tilt right

Repeat twice								
PATTERN	Right	Centre	Left	Centre	Right	Centre	Left	Centre
TIMING	**7** 2	3 4	5 6	7 8	**8** 2	3 4	5 6	7 8

centre

turn left

Repeat twice								
PATTERN	Right	Centre	Left	Centre	Right	Centre	Left	Centre
TIMING	**3** 2 3 4	5 6 7 8	**4** 2 3 4	5 6 7 8	**5** 2 3 4	5 6 7 8	**6** 2 3 4	5 6 7 8

Remember

◆ Do the warm-ups before trying the short sequences.
◆ Practise each section of the warm-ups and sequences separately before joining it onto another section.
◆ Repeat the whole task several times when you have joined all of the sections together.

Suggested music

◆ *Gentle On My Mind*, Glen Campbell
◆ *Stranger On The Shore*, Acker Bilk
◆ *True Colours*, Eva Cassidy

centre

tilt left

centre

Breathing and waist twists

1 Inhale and exhale

◆ Inhale for four seconds, raise arms up the side, palms up.

◆ Exhale for four seconds, lower arms back to original position, palms down.

◆ Repeat four times.

start position

inhale arms up

> **WARNING**
>
> If you are recovering from a slipped disc or have artificial hips, take some advice before adding the next section of this warm-up.

2 Add waist turns

◆ Sit upright on the chair, feet firmly on floor.

◆ Twist right from waist as far as you can, without turning your hips.

◆ Twist left from waist as far as you can, without turning your hips.

◆ Repeat four times (right, left, right, left, right, left, right, left).

> **TECHNIQUE TIP**
> Turn from the waist, not from your hips and make sure you pass through the centre position every time you twist.

waist twist right

waist twist left

Repeat four times								
PATTERN	Right	Left	Right	Left	Right	Left	Right	Left
TIMING	**5** 2 3 4	5 6 7 8	**6** 2 3 4	5 6 7 8	**7** 2 3 4	5 6 7 8	**8** 2 3 4	5 6 7 8

exhale arms down

Repeat four times

PATTERN	Inhale arms up	Exhale arms down	Inhale arms up	Exhale arms down	Inhale arms up	Exhale arms down	Inhale arms up	Exhale arms down
TIMING	**1** 2 3 4	5 6 7 8	**2** 2 3 4	5 6 7 8	**3** 2 3 4	5 6 7 8	**4** 2 3 4	5 6 7 8

Something harder

Add an extra stretch

◆ Add a reach across your body with your arm as you do the waist turns.

◆ Twist right, reach across with left arm.

◆ Twist left, reach across with right arm.

waist twist right   waist twist left

Adapting dance styles

Adapting tap

1 Eight toe taps

- Sit upright on the chair with feet on floor and knees at 90°.
- Lift toe of right foot then place it down strongly, hitting the 'button taps' clearly on floor and putting weight on whole of foot (toe).
- Toe left foot.
- Repeat eight times (right, left, right, left, right, left, right, left).

start position

right toe up

PATTERN	Right	Left	Right	Left	Right	Left	Right	Left
TIMING	1 2	3 4	5 6	7 8	2 2	3 4	5 6	7 8

2 Add two x stamp, stamp, step back, step back

- Stamp right foot.
- Stamp left foot, bring left foot parallel with right foot.
- Step back on ball of right foot, transfer weight onto right foot.
- Step back left foot, bring left foot parallel with right foot, weight slightly more on left foot.
- Repeat.

right foot lifted

right foot down (stamp)

PATTERN	Stamp right foot	Stamp left foot	Step back right foot	Step back left foot	Stamp right foot	Stamp left foot	Step back right foot	Step back left foot
TIMING	3	2	3	4	5	6	7	8

3 Add four stamp and brushes

- Stamp right foot.
- Lift left leg, from knee backward and swing left foot forward, so the ball quickly brushes against the floor (forward brush).
- Your heel should not touch the floor, finish with left foot off floor.
- Stamp left foot, forward brush right foot.
- Repeat.

stamp right foot

brush forward left foot

PATTERN	Stamp right foot	Brush left foot	Stamp left foot	Brush right foot	Stamp right foot	Brush left foot	Stamp left foot	Brush right foot
TIMING	4	2	3	4	5	6	7	8

right toe down

left toe up

TECHNIQUE TIP
As your ankles get stronger and looser try doing the toe taps in double time (twice as fast).

left foot stamp

step back right foot

step back left foot

HELPFUL HINT
Sew some buttons loosely onto a piece of material, attach some elastic and slip over your shoes to give a tapping sound as the buttons touch the floor.

stamp left foot

brush forward right foot

4 Repeat the sequence starting with the left foot

◆ Check that you are sitting up straight and then repeat the whole sequence, starting with your left foot.

Adapting burlesque

1 Right arm and left arm across chest

- ◆ Sit upright with feet on floor and knees at 90°, hands on hips.
- ◆ Take right arm across chest.
- ◆ Place hand on left shoulder and leave there, turn head left.
- ◆ Repeat left arm.

TECHNIQUE TIP
Use a boa or large scarf around your shoulders to help you get more into the spirit.

start position

right arm across chest
1 2

left arm across chest
3 4

3 Cross right leg over left leg and brush up body to high 'V'

- ◆ Cross right foot over left foot.
- ◆ Reach forward and draw the boa up body, look at hands.
- ◆ Finish in high 'V', look up towards right hand.
- ◆ Repeat whole sequence starting with left arm.

WARNING
Sit well back in the chair and only go as far forward as you feel comfortable. Don't go too low as you may fall out of the chair, or it may topple onto the front legs.

Suggested music

- ◆ *Fever*, Peggy Lee
- ◆ *Feeling Good*, Michael Bublé

cross right foot over left foot, reach forward
2 2 3 4

draw boa up body
5 6

2 Add taking arms to side

- ◆ Extend right arm to side at shoulder level, look along arm.
- ◆ Leave it there.
- ◆ Repeat left arm.

HELPFUL HINT

Lots of other tasks and sequences in this book could be adapted to do sitting on a chair – have a look and try some ideas. Remember not to do too much at once if you have not been active for a while.

extend right arm
5 6

extend left arm
7 8

finish high 'v'
7 8

Get dancing!

There is a growing interest in supporting more people to dance, whatever their age or physical and intellectual abilities. This book hasn't attempted to cover this area, rather to give some simple tips and ideas to get you dancing at home.

I hope you have found the book useful. If you have caught the dance bug and want to find out more about a particular style, or join a class, there are some useful addresses identified in the next section that may help. Many dance teachers work in one particular geographic area so it is always good to check local newspapers and websites to find out what is happening near you.

Glossary

Accent: Placing emphasis on a particular step or move.

Alignment: Basic positioning of the body with no displacement of the torso, so that the body works efficiently and safely.

Ampersand (&): Indicates that steps or movements are done between beats in a piece of music.

Balancé: A simple traditional waltz step, making a small jump onto one foot then briefly shifting weight to the toes of the other foot before returning to the first foot (flat-toe-flat).

Ball of foot: When heels are off the floor and weight is on the part of the foot just below the toes.

Barre: A support for dancers. The first section of ballet classes happens at the barre. It can also be used in other dance styles.

Basic step in six counts: A simple walking pattern that gives a basic structure for Argentine tango dancers.

Bop step: Step on one foot, briefly transfer weight to toes of other foot then return weight fully to first foot (flat-toe-flat).

Brush: Can be forward or backward. Bend the knee then strike the ball of the foot (tap) against the floor, then the leg raises in the other direction to follow through the movement.

Brush stamp: A brush with a stamp on the end of it.

Change step: A basic waltz step (step-side-close) can be done forward or backward, starting with either the right or left foot.

Chassé: A step-close-step pattern, included in many dance styles.

Choreography: Dance composition, set dances.

Collect: The act of drawing one foot to another to finish a step in Argentine tango.

Contra Position: One part of the body works in opposition to another.

Counting: How the beats work within a bar or phrase.

Dance belt: A thong-like piece of underwear worn by male dancers to support their genitals.

Dégagé: The disengagement or pointing of the foot in ballet, where the foot is pointed and there is no transfer of weight. Can be taken forward, backward or to the side.

Demi-plié: A small bend always done before and after jumps for elevation and safety.

Demi-pointe: Tiptoes (or heels raised as high of possible with the toes on the floor).

Double arm hold: A traditional ballroom hold where both partners face each and rest their hands on the other's upper arms. The partners need equal tension in their arms.

Double stamp: When a flamenco dancer does two stamps in the time of one beat in the music.

Embrace: Basic hold for Argentine tango where dancers' torsos touch at the leader's chest.

Enchaînement: A series of steps put together to make a phrase, or sentence of dance.

En dedans: (Inwards) Used in ballet to describe the direction of a turn when the dancer turns closing in towards the body, rather than out and away from the body (en dehors).

Figure: A collection of steps, particularly in ballroom dance.

Figures of eight: Hip movements that trace a sideways figure of eight. Vary in precise nature, depending on different dance styles

First arabesque: An arm position in ballet, where the same arm as the leg you are standing on is forward at shoulder level with the other arm at shoulder height to the side.

Flexed: Can relate to feet that are not pointed but clearly turned upwards from the ankle, or knees relaxed but not fully bent.

Flick: A sharp, quick movement, from the knee.

Floor pattern: A path followed during a sequence or routine.

Fuertes: Hard claps in flamenco made by hitting the palm of one hand with three fingers from the other, making a crisp and sharp sound.

Full-plié: A deep bend where the heels usually come off the floor.

Grapevine: Steps that move sideways, side-behind-side-front.

Glope: A stamp in flamenco. The foot hits the floor flat with equal weight on the toe and the heel.

Heel lead: A step when the heel clearly lands on the floor before the toe.

Heel stamp: A lift of the heel followed by a stamp.

Heel strut: Can be done in any direction. Place the heel on the floor and lower toe.

Hitch: Lift the leg off the floor, bent at the knee with weight on the other foot.

Hip circle: When the hips trace a circle as they move. Vary in precise nature depending on different dance styles.

Hip drop: A hip movement with the accent when one hip moves downward.

Hip lift: A hip movement with the accent when one hip moves upwards.

Hip shakes: A movement associated with Bollywood dance where the lowering of one hip displaces the other to the side.

Improvisation: Free movement in response to a piece of music or other stimulus.

Isolation: Done with different parts of the body including shoulders, hips and ribs. Only one part of the body moves, whilst the rest remains still.

Jazz hands: A move linked with theatre jazz where the hands wave very quickly with fingers stretched and wide apart.

Line of Dance (LOD): The direction that dancers travel in; important in ballroom where everyone needs to move anti-clockwise around the room.

Lotus hand position: A traditional mudra representing the lotus blossom.

Lunge: When legs are apart with one knee bent and the other straight. Weight over the leg with the bent knee.

Mudras: Hand signals used in traditional South Asian dance forms.

Natural turn: Turning to the man's right, in a clockwise direction.

Opposition: A natural way that we walk. When the right leg comes forward, the left arm comes forward, and vice versa.

Parallel: Feet hip width apart, toes facing front.

Pas de Bourrée: Simply means to run. They are neat and snappy, with small steps and weight over the toes. Can be taken in many variations.

Percussive: Movements that are preceded and followed by a pause so that each movement is separated from the next movement. A singular, sharp movement.

Pick up: A lifting and striking of the toe tap before undertaking a step, giving an extra beat.

Plié: Can be done in parallel or with legs turned out from the hips as in ballet. It is a bend of the legs where the knees always go over the toes and the body is in alignment.

Pirouette: A spin on one foot; can be clockwise or anti clockwise.

Point (Pointe): Feet are fully extended from the ankles.

Pose: A shape held still for a number of counts.

Prop: An adornment or object used to add interest to a dance.

Promenade position: When the leader's right side and follower's left side are in contact so their bodies make a 'v' position. Used in ballroom and Latin dance.

Relevé: A snatch of the feet together as you rise onto your toes, crossing feet close together.

Retiré: A position where one leg makes a triangular position (shape) with the foot resting against the other leg, usually at the knee.

Reverence: A bow or curtsey traditionally taken at the end of a ballet class.

Reverse turn: Turing to the leader's left, turning anti-clockwise.

Rise: Lifting the heels of the floor and balancing on tiptoes.

Rise and fall: The gradual rising onto the toes and lowering the heels characteristic of the waltz.

Scuff: To strike the floor with the ball of foot as it passes.

Shimmy (shoulders): One shoulder moves forward while the other moves back, can be done fast or slow.

Shimmy (hips): Hip drops done very fast so that they look like continuous movement in belly dancing.

Shoulder circle: Circle shoulder in the joint, can be done backward or forward.

Shuffle: A brush forward and backward joined together   .

Snake arms: A movement made with both arms imitating the fluidity of a snake. Can be done to the side or front of the body.

Sordas: Soft claps in flamenco made by cupping both hands and clapping.

Spine curl: A forward bend, starting with the head where the dancer tries to roll down moving one vertebra at a time. The dancer rolls up the spine in the same way.

Spring ball change: Done on the spot or travelling, making a jump onto one foot then briefly shifting weight onto the toes of the other foot before returning to first foot.

Stamp: Stepping on the flat of the foot, taking full weight.

Step: When the weight is transferred fully onto one foot, in any direction. In tap it is usually on the ball of the foot.

Stroke: A term used in burlesque when the hands brush up or down the whole body, or part of it, between movements.

Strut: Sassy walk with a feel of prancing.

Sur le cou-de-pied: When a foot is placed on the calf just above the ankle.

Swivel: A change of direction whilst on the balls of the feet.

Syncopated rhythm: A change in the beats or accents in a rhythm, so the beats that are usually unaccented, become accented. A key feature of jazz music.

Tendu: When the leg is stretched out straight, in any direction, with the tip of the toes touching the floor.

Tilt: A slant of the whole body or the head.

Time signature: Written as a fraction, the top number shows the number of beats in a bar and the bottom number shows what the beat is measured in.

Toes: When the dancer is standing on tiptoe.

Toe stamp: A lift of the toe followed by a stamp.

Toe strut: Can be done in any direction. Place the toe on the floor and lower heel.

Touch: Stand with weight on one foot, place the other next to it on the toes of the foot. There is no weight on the foot that does the touch.

Transfer of weight: Change body weight from one foot to another.

Turnout: Turnout is a key feature of ballet. Legs and feet rotate outwards from the hips, so that your knees face over your toes.

Unscrewing the light bulb: A popular Bollywood step where the hands twist, from the wrists imitating the action of unscrewing a light bulb.

Whisk: Step taking partners from closed hold position into Promenade position.

Zero position: Neutral position in Argentine tango where the weight is on one foot and the other foot ready to take the next step.

Useful contacts

American line dance
CopperKnob
www.copperknob.co.uk

Linedancer magazine
Tel 01704 392 300
www.linedancerweb.com

Argentine tango
Tango Timetable
www.tangotimetable.com

Ballet, Tap and Jazz
The British Ballet
Organisation
Tel 020 87481241
www.bbo.org.uk

**Imperial Society of Teachers
of Dancing (ISTD)**
Tel 020 7377 1577
www.istd.org

Royal Academy of Dance
Tel 020 7924 3129
www.rad.org.uk

Ballroom dance
British Dance Council
Tel 020 8545 0085
www.bdconline.org

IDTA
Tel 01273 685652
www.idta.co.uk

Belly dance
Mosaic Arabic Dance Network
Tel 0116 291 2395
www.mosaicdance.org

The Association for Arabic Dance
www.nada.uk.com

Bollywood dance
South Asian Dance Alliance
Tel 020 76913210
www.southasiandance.org.uk

Burlesque
Ministry of Burlesque
www.ministryofburlesque.com/

Flamenco dance
Spanish Dance Society
www.spanishdancesociety.org

**Umbrella organisations
supporting dance
classes for adults**
Exercise Movement and
Dance Partnership
Tel 01403 266000
www.emdp.org

One Dance UK
Tel 020 7713 0730
www.onedanceuk.org

People Dancing
Tel 0116 253 3453
www.communitydance.org.uk

HELPFUL HINT
All local authority
websites carry
information about
leisure activities and
usually include
dance classes.

Bibliography

Biddlecombe, Sarah. 'The Five Best Burlesque Dancers of all Time' *Telegraph* (26 October 2014).

De Mille, Agnes. *The Book of The Dance* (Paul Hamlyn Ltd, 1963).

Denning, Christine. *The Meaning of Tango: The Story of the Argentinian Dance* (Pavilion Books, 2008).

Du Beke, Anton. *Anton's Dance Class* (Kyle Cathie Ltd, 2007).

Hill, Constance Valis. *Tap Dancing America: A Cultural History* (Oxford University Press, 2014).

Lexova, Irena. *Ancient Egyptian Dances* (Dover Publications, 2003).

Mack, Lorrie. *The Book of Dance* (Dorling Kindersley, 2012).

Mackrell, Judith. 'How Lighting Design and Technology are Transforming Dance on Stage' *The Guardian* (4 February 2014).

Marcoux, Erica. 'The Globalisation of Bollywood Dance' www.sophia.smith.edu/blog/danceglobalization (29 April 2012).

Powell, David. 'What is Line Dancing?' www.roots-boots.net (January 2003).

Rhythm India. 'What is Bollywood?' www.rhythm-india.com/bollywood-dance.

Subramaniam, Arundhathi. 'Bollywood Dancing: Dance in Hindi Films in India' *Animated* (Autumn 2012), 25–27.

Thorpe, Edward. *Black Dance* (Chatto and Windus Ltd, 1989).

Townsend, Lucy. 'Bollywood Dance Explained' www.bbc.co.uk/news/magazine/18686742 (July 2012).

Tyldesley, Joyce. *Daughters of Isis* (Penguin, 1995).

Von Teese, Dita. *Burlesque and the Art of the Tease* (HarperCollins, 2006).

Watterson, Barbara. *Women in Ancient Egypt* (Amberley Publishing, 2011).

Wilson, Chris. *Flamenco Essentials* (Chris Wilson & UK Flamenco, 2009).

Wolter, Ruth. 'Anything Goes as Long as the Story Requires It'. http://www.digital-development-debates.org/issue-08-sport--culture--dancing-for-bollywood-anything-goes.html. (August 2012)